LIFE IN THE LEADERSHIP LANE

Moving Leaders to

Inspire and Change

the Workplace

By Bruce W. Waller

Cover and book layout design by Deanne Vick
Edited by Stacy Davis

Printed in the United States of America
First Edition 2021

ISBN - 978-0-578-90364-4

For more information, visit www.brucewaller.com

ENDORSEMENTS

"Bruce was born to speak and write about leadership. He lives his life as a true leader and, in efforts to learn from others, he engages in meaningful conversations with leaders of different organizations, backgrounds and cultures. He continuously motivates and inspires others. Any time you spend with Bruce, whether through podcast, in person, or in his books, will be well worth the investment. You will walk away energized and ready to be the best person you can be. The world needs more leaders like Bruce Waller!"

Jill Cole, Chief Human Resources Officer

"Bruce Waller has accumulated a tremendous well of leadership knowledge to draw from in his book, *Life in the Leadership Lane*. His access to leaders in all walks of life and business makes for an addicting read for someone seeking to become a better and more well-rounded leader in his/her field."

Toby Rowland, The Voice of the Oklahoma Sooners

"This book covers it all. It is a MUST read for all leaders (and by the way, we are all leaders)! It is full of insightful strategies, stories and tools to grow your impact as a leader and influencer. What a great leadership resource guide! This book would be an outstanding gift for anyone wanting to improve their leadership journey and those around them."

Bronwyn Allen, President and CEO

"*Life in the Leadership Lane* is the one-stop shop of leadership books. Filled with personal stories and great advice, Bruce takes you on a journey through building relationships, evaluating yourself against your toughest critic (you) and inspires you with anecdotes based on real life and real learning. Do yourself a favor and read this book. Then, re-read this book and keep it on your bookshelf as a go-to reference. Leadership is lonely, but it's also a community – and Bruce helps connect us on the only level that matters – the human level."

Diane Sanford, Chief People and Risk Officer

"Bruce Waller is one of the most masterful networkers and connectors I've ever seen. He does not connect just to add names to his list; each and every interaction with him is meaningful and purposeful. His book *Life in the Leadership Lane* is a blueprint on how to take your leadership game to the next level. His ability to connect with you through stories is top notch. I guarantee you will finish this book with quotes and tips that you will be eager to share with others."

Tonya Carruthers, Chief Human Resources Officer

"I am so grateful for my friend Bruce Waller; he is a courageous leader and always giving to others. In his new book he captures the true spirit of being a leader and shares how many CHRO's and other outstanding leaders have been role models of success because of their attitudes and commitment to personal growth. I know you will be inspired by *Life in the Leadership Lane*."

Lynne Stewart, President

"Bruce Waller has done it again! *Life in the Leadership Lane*, like all of his books, makes you think, reflect and leaves you wanting more! We all have the power to change, and this book may provide you with the nudge you may need. Each chapter can be read again and again and each time the reader will gain new insight. Thank you, Bruce! *Life in the Leadership Lane* is the perfect roadmap to creating a custom success plan for the reader personally and professionally."

Elizabeth Jee, Hiring Strategist

"Bruce Waller is a leader, a storyteller and the kind of person who drives others to be the best version of themselves. Throughout *Life in the Leadership Lane,* he does a phenomenal job of laying the groundwork to guide you down the lane to your best self professionally and personally. A must read if you are looking to be inspired by many voices and a wealth of experience!"

Rose Ann Garza, Chief Human Resources Officer

"*Life in the Leadership Lane* by the masterful storyteller, Bruce Waller, is a must read! While a quick read, I found this new offering to be a lot of action & not so much talk - exactly what one needs to travel the road throughout the journey in closing the gaps - current state versus where dreams are realized! Bruce, in his artful writing, charts a path to "all in" living, leading & loving that will change one's trajectory to accomplish way beyond personal & professional expectations! This author has given the greatest professional & personal gift ever possible – the voice of success & failure that inspires all levels of leaders to keep learning, growing & making impact one decision maker in their sphere of influence at a time. This new offering is the gift that will keep on giving – it is a must read!!"

Dr. Sandra Reid, Professor of Marketing

"Bruce has a unique ability to inspire simply through living his passion. Influencing leaders to become influential leaders and sharing his knowledge with all of us is his gift. We all become a little better and wiser by listening and learning from Bruce and his compilation of stories, conversations and ideas. Through every single interaction and experience he has with people, it's all met with gratitude. That kind of authenticity and humility makes me ever so grateful for the gift he gives."

Annie Carolla, Global Director of Talent Acquisition

"*Life in the Leadership Lane* is by far one of the most comprehensive books on leadership ever written. Full of cold hard facts supported by real world case studies. A great read for students to CEOs. It's a must 'Opt-in!'"

Ed Curtis, CEO

"As a true leader himself, Bruce Waller helps all of us see how we can choose to do a little better every day by being grateful, purposeful and believing in ourselves and others.

Lynn Shotwell, President and CEO

"To meet Bruce is to instantly connect with a genuinely curious, empathetic and charismatic leader who uses his platform to amplify others. Bruce's understanding of how leaders help to shape, disrupt and redefine what leadership and influence looks like in the workplace and drawing out their many valuable nuggets of wisdom in authentic conversation is a true gift that he has. In a world that continues to be fast-paced and ever-changing, Life in the Leadership Lane's simplicity and inspirational storytelling is a gem of relevant information that should be part of any leader's go-to toolbox."

Halima K. McWilliams, Inclusive Culture Consultant and Speaker

"Bruce Waller has woven together personal development stories, reflection exercises, and growth challenges that will encourage and motivate individuals, both starting their leadership journeys and those who are seasoned leaders alike, to be the person God created and intended them to be."

Lauren Truelove, VP of Administration

"Life in the Leadership Lane depicts the importance of collaboration. By striving to connect and learn from his peers Bruce Waller infuses deeper meaning into the word networking. Networking is the action or process of interacting with others to exchange information and develop professional or social contacts. Bruce illustrates the impact of taking this definition to new levels. Instead of contacts, he builds relationships that he continually nurtures. In a world that tends to focus on an individual's achievements, *Life in the Leadership Lane* portrays a community of accomplished individuals focused on the needs of others."

LaToya Whatley, Vice President of Human Resources

"Bruce Waller is truly a role model in regards to true servant leadership and character. He can speak with experience and credibility on life in the leadership lane. He puts others first in style of leadership and inspires anyone he comes in contact with to live their best life personally and professionally. If you want to enhance your trajectory personally or in your career then read *Life in the Leadership Lane* to be inspired to live your best life!"

Kelvin Goss, Senior Director of Diversity, Equity, and Inclusion

"Bruce is a natural connector of people leaders with a passion for appreciating the diverse and unique perspectives, values and experiences that make-up remarkable leadership, As we reflect on the unprecedented times of a global pandemic, a period when our country witnessed George Floyd's death and other unacceptable and tragic losses that sparked a movement to challenge the status quo, and in an environment of great political divisiveness, this has stretched and challenged all leaders. Bruce did not hide and wait - he charged forward with his curiosity to listen and learn from many who have persevered through this within their leadership lanes. So now is the time to listen, learn and reflect on the many voices of leadership that Bruce has captured within *Life in the Leadership Lane*."

Adrianne Court, Chief Human Resources Officer

"Bruce Waller takes us down a path, on a journey with effortless storytelling style and passion about the people and life lessons that bring each of us to a better place through his own choice to lead this valuable discussion. As Bruce shares his passion for leadership, he takes us on a path to realizing that life and the choices we make define who we become as leaders."

Erin McKelvey, Executive Director

"Bruce is a life lifter, the consummate encourager and cheerleader. Bruce is passionate about using his microphone, and in this case, his book, to speak his beliefs into people through stories, strategies, and resources to help them be better leaders – no matter their title. Whether you are leading yourself or leading a team, Bruce will guide you to embrace the daily choice to show up as a leader and live life in the leadership lane."

Nicole Roberts, Vice President of People & Culture

TABLE OF CONTENTS

*This book is dedicated to everyone who has inspired
or encouraged me to be better in the workplace
and to those who choose to live life in the leadership lane.*

Our workplaces and our world need you!

FOREWORD

I laid the ball down on the tenth board about ten feet out. As it skidded down the lane, it drifted to the eighth board at about forty-five feet. I knew I had thrown a good shot and was not surprised to see the ball snap into the pocket and clear the deck. Seven in a row.

I had strung seven in a row many times before, but this day was special. I had entered a men's bowling tournament and my performance not only legitimized my presence in the event, but also put me in place to advance and possibly, win a purse.

I was rolling an Ebonite Turbo and as I headed toward the approach, a friend would grin and say, "It's Turbo time!"

Approaching the eighth frame, I heard it again, "It's Turbo time!" Another strike. When I stood on the approach for the ninth frame, I could feel nervousness begin to spread throughout my body. I focused on my target forty-five feet down and concentrated on pushing the ball out onto the lane, another strike. Nine strikes in a row. This was new. I had never strung nine in a row in sanctioned play. A new kind of nervousness came over me. My friend encouraged me and said, "You can do this. You've got the line. Just put the ball out there." He was absolutely sincere even though we were competing against one another.

Walking toward the ball return, I heard it again... "It's Turbo time!" I could feel the nervousness moving from my chest down into my legs. I focused on my target, reminded myself to put the ball out at least ten feet, and threw strike number TEN. I heard a cheer from behind me. I looked back and could see numerous people who had gathered behind me to watch the final frame.

On the eleventh ball, my nervousness caused me to lay the ball down early. It failed to drift and began to bite too soon. The ball came up high in the pocket and...it carried. Eleven in a row. I heard a loud cheer from the crowd behind me.

As I stood on the approach for the out ball and, possibly, a perfect game, I could literally feel my knees shaking and I wondered if the crowd behind me could see them shaking. I focused on my target and reminded myself that I got lucky on the previous ball and it was critical to get the ball out on the lane. I can't lay it down early. I was so nervous I wasn't sure if I could start moving. I took my first step…

There was one person in the crowd behind me that was a little more nervous than me - my cheerleader who kept reminding me, "It's Turbo time!" He was nervous for me, not because he's my little brother, but because he wanted to see me succeed, to complete my first sanctioned perfect game. He would have wanted to see anyone on that approach succeed because he is a life lifter.

In his book, *Find Your Lane*, Bruce Waller describes a lifter as one who encourages another. Bruce is, and has always been, a lifter. If you have met Bruce Waller, you know this to be true. He is always looking for new ways to lift people up and connect them with one another. From *Be a Lifter Leadership Interviews* to *Life in the Leadership Lane* podcasts, Bruce is routinely seeking to learn the processes, and grow through the wisdom of top leaders, so that he may share it with others for education and growth.

This was the purpose of his first book, *Find Your Lane*. Bruce wanted to share the challenging and difficult lanes he traveled before ultimately finding the lane that resulted in real joy and fulfillment in his career. He simply wanted you to find your lane too.

In *Life in the Leadership Lane*, Bruce takes us deeper by using one of Melanie Shaffer's (CEO Talent Suite) core values, collaboration (Chapter seven). By collaborating with top leaders from many disciplines who have found their lane, Bruce has continued to grow in his leadership and career. You'll learn more about Bruce's "Growth Day" commitment in chapter two. Bruce wants to share what he's learned to inspire other leaders and change the workplace. So get ready to learn and grow, not only from Bruce, but from great leaders like Yvonne Freeman, Jennifer McClure, Lynn Shotwell, Tony Bridwell, and many others. You will also hear personal stories of overcoming adversity and how an early pivot sent Bruce on a journey he could have only imagined just a few weeks before.

Bruce continues to work hard to lift and connect others. He's a lifter and that's what lifters do. And he wants to inspire you to be a lifter too.

Mark W. Waller

INTRODUCTION

"Welcome to *Life in the Leadership Lane*. I'm your host Bruce Waller and I get to talk to leaders who make a difference in the workplace and in the community. What did they do to get started in their careers, and what are they doing to stay there?" I have connected with some of the most interesting, inspiring and energizing business leaders since starting my podcast, and this is how I open up the show each week.

Some people have asked me why I started the podcast, and why I am on a mission to serve others in the area of leadership. My story may be similar to yours, as I found myself struggling to find my lane on many occasions as a young manager. I remember the challenging times when I felt like I was on an island trying to do everything on my own. One of those times included dealing with an employee issue in which the person didn't trust me and I didn't trust her. I remember how difficult it felt, particularly because I did not really have anyone to talk to about it. I was trying to "make my mark" as the manager and thought I needed to take care of things on my own. Then I remember a time during that period when I was encouraged…and what it felt like when I was handed a John Maxwell audio tape that changed the trajectory of my career. It immediately moved me from managing my team to leading my team. A new world opened up that helped me to see how to better navigate my team in the leadership lane. It started with people and the practice of building relationships with my team, and that grew to include others I met along the way.

Since then, I have had a hunger for leadership books, tapes, and conferences. I get energized talking with leaders and learning from them. How do they lead? How do they make decisions? What drives them? It's inspiring to hear their stories, and has made me a better leader - not by copying what they do - but by using what I learn to inspire others. I later moved out of a manager role and into a sales and marketing role as a contributor, but continued to "lead from the middle."

Reflecting back, I recall a time when I was approached after a leadership presentation that I had shared. The person asked, "Bruce, why are you so passionate about leadership when you are not actually leading a team in your company?" I thought, *what a great question*, and smiled. You see, we are all in leadership. We don't have to have a title. In fact, leading ME has been and continues to be one of my biggest challenges every day.

I knew that when they asked that question, they were implying that I didn't have a team of people actually reporting to me, and this is my point. We don't have to have a team to lead. We can still serve and model behavior for others. We can still encourage and show kindness. We can still be curious and compassionate. We can still walk beside those who need someone to just listen…those who need to feel heard and understood. This is what life in the leadership lane is all about. It's how we walk with others in our everyday. We have so many opportunities to lead - as an employee, a salesperson, a receptionist, or someone in the field…or as a brother, a mother, or a dad.

When I finished college, I accepted a position in operations management and continued down this path of hiring, training, and motivating people to help move our organization forward. Years later, I decided to pivot into a sales and marketing role that gave me a new perspective. In this position, I didn't have anyone who reported directly to me, but I was still leading myself. I was also part of "sales leadership," so I was involved in mentoring and sharing best practices with others. In addition to leading at my workplace, I also led as a volunteer, serving as the President for the third largest SHRM chapter in the country, and later served as chairman of the board. Today, I continue to volunteer, helping develop HR leaders across the great state of Texas.

Leadership is a choice *every day*. Leading can happen in the workplace, in the community or in your home. As a young boy, I had made the choice to lead and serve since junior high, when I ran for student council president. It was a lot of fun and I connected well with everyone! Early in my career, as a young entrepreneur, I chose to lead the Southwest Bowling Proprietors Association, and later the North Texas Relocation Professionals (a regional relocation council for WorldwideERC, an association for relocation professionals) to educate and network with others providing relocation services across the world. Later, I chose to lead DallasHR in Dallas, Texas! Leadership can be challenging, but the rewards of helping people are worth it!

In 2017, I found another way to lead by writing and publishing *Find Your Lane.* In this book, I shared my personal career journey - the ups and downs, the struggles, the successes, and the people that helped me along the way. It was so energizing to receive feedback from others who read the book. Many people shared feedback through book reviews, emails, texts, social media posts, and some even mailed personal letters. It was moving to hear the stories about how the book encouraged them.

Since then, I have continued to pursue ways to lead and encourage others in the workplace. In 2019, I published *Milemarkers: A Five Year Journey,* a journal to help people capture the highlights of their everyday. Then in 2020, I started a podcast called *Life in the Leadership Lane* to explore the stories of workplace and community leaders. It was another way of leading - something I had wanted to do for a while, and I just had not invested the time to take action.

I knew these one-on-one conversations would be great, I just didn't realize how great. I have interviewed some of the most brilliant-minded leaders serving as CEOs, Presidents, CHROs, VPs, Managers, Directors, Sports Broadcasters, and more. Every conversation is inspiring and energizing, and these conversations continue to be an important part of my personal and professional growth. In fact, I call interview days my "growth days." They are stories, life lessons that can help us become better leaders and ultimately create acceleration in the leadership lane.

In his book, *Start with Why*, Simon Sinek says, "There are leaders and there are those that lead. Those that lead, inspire." In this book, I have share some common threads I have discovered through hosting the *Life in the Leadership Lane* podcast, that I hope will help to inspire you on your journey:

> Leaders are "on the air" by making the choice or opt in to lead.
> Leaders make growth part of their every day.
> Leaders know how to influence the process.
> Leaders are always building and shaping their brand.
> Leaders have a passion for developing future leaders.

Leaders give value and, in return, become even more valued.
Leaders are grateful for both success and failure.
Leaders grow in community.
Leaders automate systems to record each day with purpose.
Leaders use their microphone to speak their belief into people.

In this book, we are going to cover these common threads, along with many others, by sharing real life stories. This book is not about theories, but about real leaders who have taken the journey and experienced both success and failure in their careers. *Life in the Leadership Lane* is about stories, strategies, and resources to help you become a better leader, so that you can help others become better too! In Episode 60, Jennifer Swisher, Chief Human Resources Officer, said during our conversation, "Let's be better." My hope is that this book will inspire you to be better…to grow, connect, move and energize you…so you can help to change the workplace and ultimately change the world.

So, let's go!

You're on the Air

It's Growth Day

Speak Your Influence

Build Your Brand

Building Community Networks

Turn It Up

Showing up with Gratitude

Recording with Purpose

Mic Up with Belief

Five Star Advice

Take the Challenge

CHAPTER 1

You're on the Air

"Just because you don't have a certain title
doesn't mean you're not a leader."
LaToya Whatley

For my last birthday, my wife gave me an electric sign to use for the *Life in the Leadership Lane* podcast that reads, "LIVE ON AIR." It lights up and is a great backdrop for the video podcast, so it's super energizing and exciting to have in the show. As I reflect on this leadership concept, I think about how we are always "on the air" in the workplace, in our community, in an interview, at a networking event, on a zoom call, in the grocery store, out with friends, when posting social media, and everywhere we go. We are on the air in our homes with our family too! On the air is basically saying I have prepared or not prepared for the day and how I show up. Unfortunately, it's not our choice whether or not we are "on the air," but it is our choice about how we show up. It is our choice to be prepared, to lead or not to lead, and to engage or disengage in our everyday. As you read this book, think about how you are "on the air" and what you might do to create a great experience for anyone and everyone in your path. When you choose to do this, you are truly living life in the leadership lane.

I thoroughly enjoy connecting on the podcast with leaders who are making an impact, partially because it's recorded, and something we can share to help others across the globe. During my interview with Vice President of HR, Halima K. McWilliams on Episode 40, she shared her perspective about the importance to "Opt In" during our conversation about diversity in the workplace. It was an epiphany! According to Halima, when we see something that we want, we can choose to *subscribe* in order to stay connected to the information, because we enjoy it or we want to be a part of something that will help us get better. She didn't say everyone is going to be part of it, she said people could "choose" to opt in! When we get to make the choice, we value it more.

However, there are times when we find ourselves opting out or hitting the "unsubscribe" button because we didn't sign up for it or didn't want to be part of the group, the conversation, the new project, job changes, relationships, etc. - and that's okay. It's our choice. We are all in a different season and there can be many reasons why we decide *not* to opt in. Just a few examples include already having the product or service, not having the time for it right now, or not feeling it adds value for us.

How often do you find yourself "opting in" or subscribing to a new newsletter or blog? Do you unsubscribe more than you subscribe, because someone included you on their mailing list? I enjoy subscribing to something new because it gives me energy, knowing it will add value in my career. I also find myself unsubscribing to things that do not add value – and it can be annoying and draining, having to go through the process.

Leadership is a choice too. It's a choice for each of us to "opt in" every day! It doesn't matter what role you are in - HR, Sales, Customer Service, Project Management, Finance, Payroll, Administration, fill-in-the-blank. We have the choice to lead every day - starting with leading ourselves!

One of the things I appreciate the most about my guests who appear on a *Life in the Leadership Lane* podcast is that they have all "opted in" to share their stories. Stories energize me and I always find myself wanting to know more about their stories. Where did they grow up? How did they get started in their careers? What energizes them? It is always fascinating and often validates or provides reflection for me in my journey. I have found that it is very common for leaders who have enjoyed success to be in a totally different place than they had originally planned. In fact, many people will say something like, "I fell into this role/industry." Like many others, I also fell into my career of serving others in relocation. I started on bowling lanes, working with my mom and dad, before I moved to Texas to begin a long career in the relocation lane. I was enjoying my role as a young manager in the bowling and recreation industry but wanted to align more with who I wanted to become as a husband, father, and professional. When I decided to make a change, I "opted in" to conversations with others to help guide me on my path. It was challenging, because it was not only about leadership in my career, but also within my family and more importantly - within myself.

Over the years, I have "opted in" to many conversations about changes in my career, my volunteer roles, and more. I haven't always subscribed to a change, but I have always opted in to the conversation about leading. I always wanted to be "in the conversation." When we opt in, we are saying, "I'm interested in hearing more, seeing if this will add value and if so, I am all in." If not, we can choose to opt out.

It's great to always keep our eyes and ears open for these opportunities, but it can be challenging if we take on too much. This can cause us to lose focus on what's most important. I mean we only have so much time in the day, right? One of the ways I try to stay focused on what's most important is having a "Yes" and a "Not Yet" list. The "Yes" list includes my top 3-5 goals for the year, and my "Not Yet" list includes everything that doesn't support my goals. It's not saying I don't want to opt in, I am just saying not yet. For example, I might glance at my website and realize I need to update or make some changes, but it's not something I can fit in my schedule at the time. In this case, I will add *update website* to my "Not Yet" list. This always allows me to capture the information to review again at a later date. I keep this close by so that when I think about something, I can just add it to the list and approach it when the time is right. When I review, I see that my "Yes" list stays smaller for focus, and the "Not Yet" list gets really long.

So, what are you going to OPT IN to this week? Will you start a conversation about something stirring your heart, start a new blog, join a new association, fill out a volunteer application, sign up to be a speaker, apply for a new job, ask for a new role, ask for a raise, attend a Zoom invite, join a book club, make a call, make a new connection?

Remember, you're on the air… So, make the choice to "opt in" to drive in the leadership lane and make a difference!

How Are You Showing Up?

One of my conversations on *Life in the Leadership Lane* podcast was with Senior Global Talent Acquisition manager Jimmy Richards (Episode 68) when we talked about the importance of *showing up in the workplace*. We talked about candidates looking for a new role. He shared that soft skills are transferrable in every industry, and that most employers are looking for these skills to *show up* during the interview. Some of those skills include passion, energy level, ability to influence, humility, vision and communication. You can also include being a team player, being adaptable, and having empathy. How we show up makes a difference. In fact, CEO Satya Nadella noted empathy as one of the most important skills we can have in the workplace in his book, *Hit Refresh*.

How do you show up for the following events?

> *Work meeting*
> *Lunch with a client or friend*
> *Networking event*
> *Volunteer event*
> *Family events*
> *Out with friends*
> *In your community*
> *Virtual meeting*
> *Conference*
> *Interviewing for your next job*

You see, it doesn't matter what the event is because we are *always* on the air. We are always being interviewed or making decisions based on these soft skills. We don't have a choice about being on the air, but we do have the choice of how we show up. So, what can you change today that will help you to stand out in your role? Remember, *you're on the air*!

Sometimes We Need to Reset

I can hear her voice just like it was yesterday. "Reset on lane seven." Her name was Mabel Carter and she bowled the afternoon senior league. She wasn't even 5 feet tall, and had blond hair with wire frame glasses. Every time she threw her 8 lb. clear bowling ball down the lane, it would roll so slow that it wouldn't hit the pins hard enough to trigger the reset. Then she would shout, "Reset please!" Many times, I helped her push the reset button, and other times I had to run to the back of the lanes and manually flip the clutch to reset the lanes. It would sweep off the pins that she knocked down, so she could roll her second ball.

Resetting is also a great time to reflect on what's most important to you. I believe that when we choose to reset, we choose to be purposeful in evaluating where we are in our career and where we want to go. Some people do this weekly, monthly or annually when reviewing goals.

When I first started thinking about hosting a leadership podcast, it just wasn't the right time or season. I have always been fascinated by leaders who make a difference in the workplace or in their community. How did they get to where they are? What habits, disciplines or practices do they focus on each day to help them keep growing in their leadership? My initial plan was to visit each different workplace, interview using my phone, and call it "Leaders on the Street." It was a fun idea, but I had so much going on that I didn't feel like I could sustain it for a long period of time. I was writing my book at the time, so I just added it to my "not yet" list for a later season in my career.

Fast forward to March 2020, when the world changed as the coronavirus pandemic arrived and many of us were forced to work from home. Technology companies ramped up, helping us all stay connected in the workplace. I decided to hit the reset button! I wrote down all of the things I was doing at the time and all of the things I wanted to do, which included staying connected to others in my profession. I decided to start my podcast, calling it *Life in the Leadership Lane*. In 2022, I will eclipse the 100-episode mark, with an audience of more than 20 countries from around the world.

It's exciting to have dialogue with different leaders and learn what they are doing to make a difference, as well as help others who are tuning in to the show. You see, there are many strategies to success. We just need to find our lane and the inspiration that works best for us!

So, what are you doing to reset? What about resetting your role in the workplace? Are you spending time or investing time on yourself to get better in your career? Are you expanding your network? Consider "opting in" to join a virtual networking group in your industry, to learn more and stay connected. Chief People Officer Steve Browne (Episode 48) talked about the importance of volunteering in our industry to change our profession. When we volunteer, we connect, engage, and learn different perspectives to bring to our organization and to our career.

Find someone that inspires you and opt in to a conversation with them. Find out what they do, what they value, how they spend their time, and who is in their networking groups. Then take a step to reset and opt in for your next move.

What Energizes You?

The last 5-10 minutes of every podcast interview, I have a segment called *It's Time to Accelerate* where I ask a few last-minute questions to get to know my guests on a personal level. As I prepare, I am always looking for different questions to bring out more of the guest's personality. I like to share these questions ahead of time, to give them time to reflect and think about what they might say. Yvonne Freeman (Episode 15) shared a different question that she liked when it comes to favorite hobbies or things we like to do with our spare time. The question is, "*What energizes you?*" The way she framed it was energizing, and I immediately implemented her question into the show. It's impactful...because it's more than asking about what hobbies we enjoy, it's about what

When we identify what energizes us, it helps us find our passion and leads to more opportunities ahead.

makes our heart sing! When we are energized, we become interested and passionate about it. When we know what energizes us, we can get in better alignment with our purpose because we know what makes us feel most alive. When we are around things or people that energize us, we feel joy, we feel love, and we have a sense of fulfillment in our life.

Later that week, I went through a reflection process to identify the things that energized me. I grabbed a pen and a sheet of paper and started writing down all of the things that energize me and posted on my blog. It's such a great exercise, in every season of life, to reflect on these things. When we identify what energizes us, it helps us to find our passion and leads us to more opportunities ahead.

So, what energizes me?

- *Learning something new*
- *Sharing ideas*
- *Interviewing guests for my podcast*
- *Winning business opportunities*
- *Watching college football with family and friends*
- *Speaking at an industry event*
- *Networking*
- *Family reunions*
- *Building new partnerships*
- *Feeling gratitude*
- *Dinners with family/friends*
- *Talking bowling with mom*
- *Connecting on social media*
- *Helping a family reduce stress for a relocation*
- *Adding value as a volunteer leader*
- *Spending time with my grandchildren*
- *Playing golf with family and friends (really energized when I play good)*

These are just a few of the things I came up with… See anything in common? *People!*

With my focus on leadership, that naturally led me to the question, *do leaders know what energizes team members*? During my interview with Yvonne, she said "people energize me." It was super inspiring, as I had noticed how well she connects with people in her path.

Look around and you can tell which leaders are energized by people. Herb Kelleher, former CEO at Southwest Airlines, was known for remembering employees' names. Frank Blake, former CEO at Home Depot, wrote over 25,000 letters during his 7 years of leading the company. They understood what energized them!

In Bob Chapman's book, *Everybody Matters*, he states that an estimated 88% or 130 million people - *7 out of 8 people* - go home feeling that they work for an organization that doesn't listen or care. Have you ever felt this way? What changed? I felt this way as I led an organization in 2002. It was really a challenging time. I needed to make some changes in my staff and I needed more resources to achieve our goals...but nobody listened. They said, "Work with what you have." It was a painful time as the leader. I was de-energized! And as I ran out of energy, I made a change! I decided to do everything I could to inspire others in my path. We all have opportunities to inspire and serve every day. We just need to make the choice to do it. When we do, it not only energizes you, it also energizes everyone around you. It's all about people!

So...what energizes you? But more importantly, what energizes your team members, your family, or your friends? Discover this, and you will unlock the door to move leaders to inspire and change the workplace!

We All Need Some "mo"

I have been a big fan of John Maxwell books for years. When he talks about the importance of momentum, it resonates with me. You see, when we have momentum, we feel like we are better than we are, and when we don't have it, we feel like we are worse! Building momentum as a leader can be challenging because it takes consistent action every day. Some days we don't feel like doing the hard stuff, but leaders do it anyway or lose the momentum they have built.

I remember attending a Zig Ziglar conference in Dallas many years ago. Zig stood on stage with an old water pump handle and talked about "priming the pump." He said that when we move the handle back and forth, it creates pressure to push water out and the more the handle is moved back and forth, the more pressure when the water eventually comes out. However, if we stop moving the handle back and forth, we lose all the pressure and have to start over.

Momentum is the same thing. When we choose to improve or *get better*, it's like moving that handle or priming the pump to build momentum. When we have momentum, we have more confidence, and we feel like we can do anything.

So how do we build momentum? Make the decision to start! OPT IN to take action, and put one foot in front of the other. It's that easy. You see, momentum doesn't stay with us for a long time. It comes and goes during the season. Build some "mo" by:

1. OPTING IN to start - someday is today.
2. Make a plan - don't wait for perfection.
3. Take action - small things lead to big things.
4. Find your why - find a coach or accountability partner.

The challenge is the start/stop phase. When we start, we begin building mo. When we stop, it all goes away, and we have to start over. The key is to start, and don't stop for anything!

Want a new job or promotion? Make a plan! Want a certification? Complete the application! Want to write a book? Start writing! Want to build a network? Make a connection! Want to run a 5K? Start jogging!

It's easy to do and - at the same time - NOT easy to do. It takes work every day. We can start building momentum one step at a time! It's exciting to know that in three months - or maybe three years - you'll look back and thank yourself for making the decision to start! The greatest part is the story you will share with others one day about the best decision you ever made, and how proud you are that you kept going! You're on the air my friend, and it's time to OPT IN for greatness!

Make Your Mark

Years ago, when I graduated from college and decided to make a career change, it involved making the decision to leave our family business and relocate to Dallas, Texas to start something new. I had no idea how special this journey was going to be. I remember the excitement about the road ahead and how nervous I was on my first day of work. As a young manager, I trained that summer on the front line as part of the moving crew. I learned to pack boxes and load furniture. One of the things I realized was that in order to be efficient, it required skill to load and unload the moving trucks. I also discovered how challenging it was to carry pianos and move sofas and other furniture up multiple flights of stairs in the heat of the summer! Yikes! In fact, my local operations manager even persuaded me to get a CDL (commercial driver license) so I could supervise my own moving crews as the lead driver. Before I knew it, I was driving all over the city and state helping families relocate. Once I completed my training, I then moved into the office to lead a team for our company. After that, I moved on to leading in the company as a general manager, and I now serve as a sales leader for one of the largest moving companies in the US.

During this time, I remember thinking on many occasions that I "wished" I would have done something special with my career after graduating college. I got depressed when I thought about how I ended up "just being a mover" and how other people were doing things like working in the medical field, or practicing law, or teaching and coaching sports to make an impact on people's lives. I hadn't really expressed this to anyone until now...but as I realized how many people might have similar thoughts, it made me want to share my story. Because it hit me...I *was* doing something special in my career. I was helping people by building relationships, developing trust, and reducing stress during one of the most stressful times of their life.

When people move, they go through many emotions - fear, anxiety, uncertainty, insecurity and more. I have experienced families that are excited about the new city and job ahead, and families who are emotionally crushed because they are leaving loved ones behind. When I realized how much I could help people during this transition, that is when I shifted my focus. I started focusing less on me and my job and more on the people relocating and their needs. The same thing happened when I decided to volunteer. I focused more on adding value for others and less on what I needed in order to have success. Then I found ways to add value though teachable moments on my blog, which later turned into a book!

You see, we all have an opportunity to make our mark as a leader in any career we choose. We just have to OPT IN and make the choice to look for ways to serve others. It may be through writing, speaking, or volunteering time to help an organization. As a leader, we need to always be asking the questions, "How can I be a better resource for

When we opt in to look beyond our world and into the world of others, that is when we start making our mark as a leader and finding joy in our career.

people in my path? What is something I can share with someone today that will help them with a challenge they are facing? As a volunteer, how can I make maximum impact?" We all have incredible strengths that can positively impact people. We just have to be intentional and make the decision to start using them for that purpose.

When we opt in to look beyond our world and into the world of others, that is when we start making our mark as a leader and finding joy in our career.

Choose Wisely

Choose to lead.

Choose to adapt.

Choose to be open-minded.

Choose to grow.

Choose to volunteer.

Choose to set the expectations.

Choose to listen.

Choose to share.

Choose to be available.

Choose to mentor.

Choose to collaborate.

Choose to inspire.

Choose to partner.

Choose to be receptive.

Choose to be kind.

Choose wisely… Every choice can help to shape the decisions for others in our organizations!

 What's Your Take?

Now that you are "On the air", what choices do you need to make to show up, to better engage, and to build momentum? Maybe you need to reset and start priming the pump once again. Do you know what energizes you? Is it people, encouragement, feedback, events, work? Write your answers down and start keeping track. Look for patterns or connections between the answers.

You're on the Air

It's Growth Day

Speak Your Influence

Build Your Brand

Building Community Networks

Turn It Up

Showing up with Gratitude

Recording with Purpose

Mic Up with Belief

Five Star Advice

Take the Challenge

CHAPTER 2

It's Growth Day

"It's not the product, it's the finished
product that matters the most."
Martha E. Thornton

I was incredibly energized and excited to finally begin interviewing leaders in my network on air for the *Life in the Leadership Lane* podcast. I was scheduling weekly recordings. I had just published my first episode with Kevin Dawson, host of *Leaders and Lagers* podcast, and I was set to interview culture expert and keynote speaker, Greg Hawks, for Episode 2. Greg had started a new feature called "Weekly Huddles" which was all about connecting people to network, learn, and grow from ideas or challenges presented. I was anxious to talk to Greg about the success of this new adventure. My goal was to learn as much as I could and share it with the world through the podcast recording to help others.

As I began the interview, I hit record…or at least I thought I did! Greg is a high-energy guy and we were having a great conversation about how he got started in business. About 15 minutes into the recording, I looked up and realized that the podcast wasn't recording. I thought…*Oh no! What do I do?*

Greg is a busy leader and I knew my time with him was limited. As he was sharing his thoughts about culture, I had to interrupt him to let him know that I didn't hit the record button and that we would have to start over. Ugh! It was really embarrassing, but thankfully Greg understood and allowed me to start the conversation over. Since then, I know the importance of double-checking the recording status before beginning the show! I share this story because life in the leadership lane is not only about success, it's about failure too. In fact, most leaders will share stories about failure and how it led them to where they are today. We all fail, and it is our choice to decide if we lay down or get back up to embrace it and use it as a learning experience.

Living life in the leadership lane is about a never-ending pursuit to grow by learning from others. We can all learn so much when we approach each day as a day to grow. We can grow by listening, being curious, being present, and drawing from our experiences. It's about having a growth mindset over an "I already know that" mindset. The best part is - the more we grow, the more we can help others grow.

Have you ever failed at something and ended up better because of it? What was it that helped you overcome failure? Many times we fail and struggle to get past the failure, but getting through failure is truly a key to driving in the leadership lane. I have found that the easiest way to bounce back from failure is to surround yourself with people who lift you with encouragement. If you find yourself in a struggle with getting past failure, change the station and listen to the voices of encouragement. Then make this lesson a growth part of your everyday!

I remember many conversations that have stood out in my career, when something was said that just *stuck*. Sometimes it was a quote, advice, or just something that was relatable and created a moment. I remember asking Talent Acquisition Leader, Ray Kallas (Episode 21), to join me on the show to share his perspective about leadership. During the show, he shared a story about one of his favorite songs called "Better Boat" by Kenny Chesney. I later downloaded the song and it's now one of my favorites! It's a song that was written following a hurricane in the Florida area. During our conversation, Ray shared that there are many things that we cannot control, and explained how he tries to focus on just getting better every day. Here are a few of the lyrics in the chorus that he shared on the show:

> *Now and then I let it go*
> *Around the waves I can't control*
> *If it's working I don't know*
> *But I can't down, the thing may not flow*
> *But I'm to build a better boat*

Look the song up and listen… It's such a great message and perspective, and it shifts our focus to growth.

Life in the leadership lane is about growing every day. In fact, I call every "one-on-one" conversation that I have with others my "growth day." I learn so much when I lean in and listen. During my conversation with CHRO Mitch Beckman in Episode 22, he shared the importance of *listening* as a leadership trait. When asked about how we can develop more influence, he said, "We need to listen, understand, relate, and listen more."

It is something we have to practice in order to get better. Many times, we already know what we are going to say before the person we are listening to is finished talking. We aren't listening and people recognize this. I am continually growing in this area myself. I've had a hunger for learning since the day I started reading and listening to leadership audio tapes. It's inspiring to listen to people's stories and it's a bonus when we can apply something from the experience to our own life.

Do you have a strategy to grow every day? Are you intentional about reading books or connecting with people? It's never too late! I would encourage you to be intentional by making every day a growth day!

Are You Asking the Right Question?
"You did it!" This is what I said to myself as I finished my run that morning. I had just completed week 9, day 3, which consisted of 4 miles. You see, it had been 10 weeks since I decided to download the C25K app and start running. The C25K app *(which stands for "Couch to 5k")* is designed to help you run 3.1 miles after 8 weeks. I saw some friends posting results on social media. Then my friend Karen, an HR leader in South Carolina, mentioned that she was using the app. With all the hype, I thought it might be worth trying. I had always wanted to run more, but I had struggled to be consistent.

I remember running my first week, in March, starting with one-minute intervals - jog one minute, then walk two minutes, and repeat this for 20 minutes. It wasn't that bad, and it created momentum for me to keep going to week two, then week three. I remember thinking, *how long will it be before I start enjoying the run? Will I make it to week eight and run a 5K?* I had run a 5K before, but this was different. I wanted to develop a habit of running. When I got to week 8, I was so proud of myself for finishing, and then I thought... *What now? Do I download the C10K app and keep going further, or stop and move on to something else?*

It's a big commitment to keep going. After all the work and investment it took to get through 8 weeks, I didn't want to lose the momentum, so I decided to keep going. As I was running week nine, it occurred to me that I was now running four miles and *enjoying* it. Then I wondered...*How far I can go?*

You see, this is what happens with many of us. It doesn't matter if it's in the workplace, in the community, or in our home. We often ask the wrong question. *How long is this going to take?* We need to shift our thinking and our question to *How far can we go? How good can we get?*

I once heard Simon Sinek talk about the infinite mindset. "When we have a finite mindset, we get to the end and it's over." For example, when we get promoted to become the HR Manager or Director, we then think *now what?* Or we achieve our year-end sales goal or land that big account, we think *now what?* Or we become the president of an organization or an association and think *now what?* It has an end! However, with an infinite mindset, the game never ends. We are always looking for ways to get better, to keep growing.

I want to challenge you to ask yourself this question... *How far can I go? How much can I grow?* You see, with the infinite mindset, we know it's not the end when we get promoted or achieve a goal – it's just the beginning of the next chapter. When we become President of an association and our term ends, this question allows us to keep looking for ways to add value and continue serving. When we graduate from college, we continue to invest in learning and growing during our career. When helping a family relocate, it's about helping to create another great experience, and always looking for ways to improve the service and outcome. The road to success never ends. In fact, many of the people on the *Life in the Leadership Lane* podcast are very successful business leaders, and share a common outlook. They are all continuous learners, looking for ways to grow and keep getting better in their careers.

Know Your Why

When I have a "growth day," it energizes me because I know that I am going to learn something that I can share with others in my network. I have been investing in growth since my brother handed me a John Maxwell tape, many years ago, to help me in my leadership journey. I remember listening to the tape and being inspired to be better. It gave me a hunger for more. Since then, I have invested in books, conferences and more. When my company offered a program, I invested. When I learned about a conference or event, I invested. It soon became part of my every day! In fact, I have identified continuous improvement as a personal value. When I am growing, I am energized. When I'm not, I feel sluggish!

In the spring of 2020, many people shifted to working from home offices due to the worldwide coronavirus outbreak. Since companies were no longer allowing people in the building for onsite speaking and training events during this time, many speakers and trainers started creating and sharing more content for training online…more than ever before, and most of it was free! A business partner and friend, Elizabeth Jee, reached out to see if I would be interested in taking an online course that was offered by Jeffrey Gitomer with her. It was called *The New Normal* and was designed to help us continue to grow during a challenging time. I had enjoyed Gitomer's books and thought some of the content could help me grow during an unprecedented time, so I agreed. I knew it would be both fun and informative. The world was changing to a virtual environment, and I needed to keep up with the change!

We scheduled weekly calls every Friday at 6:30AM, for 20 weeks! Yep, 6:30AM - so we could get it to fit in our busy schedules! Here is the thing…we are all busy, but if it is something that is going to help us grow and become more, then we need to find a way to make it happen. It might mean getting up earlier each day or working on the weekends. In order to grow, in order to become more, we must be willing to make sacrifices and put in the work. Life will happen… and it's up to us to decide if it will happen *to* us or *for* us. Most of the time, it's a short-term sacrifice for long term gain!

The following year, I decided to invest in a *Growth Day* course offered by Brendon Burchard. Brendon is one of the most popular speakers and trainers for personal development. I knew a lot of the material from reading his books and listening to his podcasts. However, he often shares key insights or perspectives in a way that helps us to look at things in a different light each time we read it or listen to it. To grow takes a personal investment, but there is no better return for our career!

> *To grow takes a personal investment, but there is no better return for our career.*

During the *Life in the Leadership Lane* podcast, I often ask guests about professional growth. Many companies have leadership development programs, but not all of them do. Some require leaders to seek their own professional development. So I ask about this topic and what advice they have for people who don't have the opportunity for professional development.

"What advice would you share with others who don't have a leadership development program, for how to grow in their careers?"

I have received some great responses. Vice President of Human Resources, Suzanne Myers (Episode 41), once shared that the first question she would want to ask is *what have you researched?* I love this because it puts the ownership back on the individual. You see, leadership growth is up to us. There is so much offered online today, especially in the LinkedIn learning community. The key to growth day is that we have to be *intentional* about it *every day*. In fact, there is so much learning available today that it often feels overwhelming, and we can get sucked into a vortex, to the point where we get burned out on learning. It takes focus and discipline to grow every day.

There have been numerous studies around success in the area of development. The following actions help achieve success with personal and professional growth:

1. Write down the goal.
2. Partner with someone who will go on the journey with us.
3. Know why it matters.

We have a better chance of success with wellness, work projects, and more when we have these things!

> *So, are you growing every day? How have you invested in YOU lately?*
>
> *It's time to start growing again!*

Moving the Chains in the Workplace

One of my favorite college football games every year is Bedlam. It's the intrastate rivalry between Oklahoma and Oklahoma State. Many families in the great state of Oklahoma have a "house divided" in which some family members pull for one team and others pull for the other team. I have family who went to Oklahoma and others who attended Oklahoma State. It's often tense and exciting as we are each hoping our team comes out on top for bragging rights. The 2020 season was no different and was intense once again.

In the 2nd half, as Oklahoma led by two touchdowns, I kept thinking about how they just needed to "move the chains" as they tried to close out the game. Oklahoma didn't need a long pass or breakaway play, just plays that could get them 3-4 yards and keep the clock moving to stay in control of the game. When you consistently make 3-4 yards per play, it leads to a first down which ultimately lets you keep the ball until you get to the end of the field for the score.

This is how high performers do it as well. They focus on moving the chains every day. Moving the chains isn't about quantum leaps, but about small actions, good choices, and having the discipline to do the little things consistently over time.

The common thread? They develop good habits and a system to help them move the chains each day. They make the decision to show up, they are open to learn, they apply what they learn, and they share it with others. They are also committed to become more by getting up early, taking care of their health, and time-blocking what's important. They are disciplined to do this to keep them on track every day. It's simple, it's tough…but it's effective.

When we develop good habits and have a system in place, growing in any role becomes easier. Growth becomes part of our day.

- *Want a promotion? Get better every day by designing a personal development plan.*
- *Want to grow your network? Schedule time to connect each day.*
- *Want to write a book? Apply the habit of writing every day with a blog by creating a system to keep you on track.*
- *Want to be a speaker? Enroll in Toastmasters to get started and practice.*
- *Want to sell more? Start investing time to create and practice conversations.*

When I started my career with Armstrong Relocation, I wanted to grow in my business. I knew that also meant I needed to grow myself as a business leader. To get started, I designed a personal development plan for myself that included reading books, improving my communication skills, and investing in my network. I knew that if I wanted to become more, I needed to invest in my communication skills. An example of this happened when my boss recommended that I enroll in a Toastmasters club to practice my presentation skills. I had heard of Toastmasters when I was in college. It is a global organization with local chapters, and is designed to help people develop their public speaking skills. I researched to find a Toastmasters club in my area.

I selected one that I could attend every week, and that is what I did for the next 100 weeks…which is more than 2 years of practicing as a speaker. It was challenging getting started, challenging in the middle, and challenging to continue – even in the end. There were many times when I was busy, or didn't feel like going, but I went anyway. Being intentional about growth can be challenging, but it is easier when we have a clear "why."

I remember applying to speak with many organizations early in my career, and not getting much interest. But I kept working at it and found that the more I spoke, the more I improved. It gives me energy when I find out someone has applied something that I shared, and it has helped them get better. Yes, there are going to be times when we are going to make mistakes, get intercepted, fumble the ball, or even come up short of the first down marker. But when this happens, and it will happen, we just need to get up and go back to the little things – the every day. One day someone will ask how you did it, and you will have the chance to think back and share the story of how you were able to move the chains in the workplace and in your life.

The Day I Missed My Appointment

Preparation is the key to success. My kids heard me share this many times at the dinner table as they were growing up. I think I heard this statement at a leadership conference early in my career and it just stuck. I remember how I felt when I was prepared, and how I felt when I wasn't. Preparation is a skill that can be learned and mastered, and helps us to advance in our careers. It is what I call a "momentum maker." You see, the higher we climb in our career, the more responsibility we take on, and the more prepared we will need to be in order to have success. It is expected! Do you remember walking into class in high school or college when you hadn't prepared for the assignment - or worse - a pop quiz or exam? YIKES!! I know I do. It was filled with negative emotions, a lack of confidence, a lack of belief, and lots of anxiety.

I also remember a time, earlier in my career, when I wasn't prepared. On that day, I looked at my calendar and got sick to my stomach. I realized that I had just missed a survey appointment to help a customer with his upcoming move. While I was trying to figure out how this happened, I wondered why the customer didn't call to ask about the surveyor and find out why I didn't show up. It was embarrassing, and I felt awful. The thought crossed my mind to just not worry about contacting him and move on…but I couldn't do that. Instead, I committed to help and decided to just call and apologize.

I told the customer how sorry I was that I had missed the appointment and that I really didn't have any excuse other than I just missed it. I knew he would be upset. I assumed he would inform me that he would be using someone else, since he couldn't depend on me. I also mentioned that if he was willing, I would like to have another chance because I knew we could provide a great move experience.

It's the little things that ultimately lead us to the big things.

I was surprised when the customer told me that he would give me a second chance. He went on to tell me the surveyor from the competition didn't show up either. What are the odds of that? I couldn't believe it. I went from being embarrassed to feeling relieved, knowing that I had owned my mistake and was given another opportunity because of it.

Preparation is a discipline. It gives us confidence, which leads to action, which leads to momentum, and ultimately leads to success. The more prepared we are, the more success we experience. However, in order to make preparation part of our everyday, we need to create a system. In other words, we need to try to automate our daily disciplines or habits that remind us to do little things every day, every week, and every year so we don't have to think about what we need to do every day. It becomes automated. It's the little things that ultimately lead us to the big things.

As the host for *Life in the Leadership Lane* podcast, I ask high-performers to share a daily practice that helps keep them on track. I have learned that they all share a common thread…and that common thread is that they have a system. Some call it a routine, I call it a system. They don't necessarily do the same things, but they all do things each day in a systematic way, from waking up early to quiet time, to reading, to time-blocking, etc.… it's their everyday!

Here are a few suggestions for automating a system that will help build your confidence and get you prepared for the next opportunity ahead.

1. Create a weekend reflection time… This should take about 20-30 minutes. Start by looking back at the previous week and write

down the things that went well and that didn't. Look for the good and you'll see the good. It's energizing!

2. Plan your calendar for the upcoming week. This should take 15-30 minutes. Block time for everything and be okay to flex when needed. Making calls, holding meetings, connecting, preparing for a presentation...everything. It will help you discern different choices to make when they come up during the week.

3. Create "Friday Finishers." This should take 10-15 minutes. I got this idea from my growth day class. On Saturday or Sunday, write down your most important weekly goals that you *must* get done - no matter what - and finish by Friday! It keeps our eyes on our most important projects.

Tom Brady, Quarterback for the Tampa Bay Buccaneers, recently won his 7th Super Bowl at the age of 43. I was reading about his preparation. He's the oldest player in the NFL and continues to play at a high level because of his preparation. He starts early every morning with study, practices every day, and is selective about the foods that he eats - no sugar, flour, etc... We don't ever see the daily struggles, only the touchdown passes! It's all in his preparation and the systems he has that provide him support for continued success. It's not easy, but it's easier with a system in place!

What is something you do each week to prepare? Do you have an everyday routine or system? How do you stay on track?

Be "All In"

I was recently invited to speak at the Lake Dallas High School Football team breakfast to kick off the new season. It's always special and an honor to share leadership lessons with young people - especially to kickoff a new season. I shared a recent article I had read about a high school quarterback, a sophomore from west Texas. He threw a pass to the wide receiver. Unfortunately, the ball slipped out of the receiver's hands and landed in the hands of an opposing defensive player's hands for an interception. The quarterback ran down the defensive player and tackled him to the ground, injuring his own shoulder in the process. The quarterback was never able to throw the same way after the injury.

After his senior season, he received a couple of division two opportunities to play football, but this kid from west Texas decided to walk-on to a school about an hour away from him in Lubbock, Texas. While at Texas Tech, he asked a lot of questions, I mean *a lot* of questions. He was very curious about everything on the field, always quizzing his coach, Mike Leach. A couple of coaches walked up to coach Leach and asked him why he was keeping this kid around, because he really wasn't good enough to make the team. Coach Leach said that he really liked the way he asked lot of questions, and he was hoping his curiosity would rub off on to the other players around him. He eventually let the young quarterback know that he wouldn't make the team as a player, but he would like to make him a student coach at age 19. A few years later, coaching changes were made and the defensive coordinator went on to be a head coach at East Carolina. The first call he made was to make this young coach his new offensive coordinator at age 27.

In 2015, Bob Stoops was looking to revamp his offense at Oklahoma when he noticed East Carolina making impact. He started researching this young offensive coach and decided to hire him at age 33. Two years later, he received an offer to be the head coach at the University of Oklahoma at age 35. His name is Lincoln Riley, and he is now considered one of the most prominent coaches in the country.

High performers choose to be great, choose to sacrifice, and choose to be intentional in their leadership growth. Those who experience significant success, such as Lincoln Riley, have many common threads, but the one that stands out is that they are ALL IN. All in is a commitment. We need to be committed in every area - family, friendships, career decisions, and community involvement - to be in growth mode.

My friend Gian Paul Gonzalez says being ALL IN is like playing poker. When you have a great poker hand and push all of your chips to the center of the table, you are saying *I am all in*, and there is no turning back. Many times, we think about being all in, but then try to pull our chips back when we realize it might not be the best hand. If we were to do this in the poker game, we just might get punched in the face for trying to pull back. What do you need to do to go ALL IN?
Gian Paul Gonzalez says, *"Commitment is not a feeling, it's an action."*

What's in Your PGP?

Do you have a personal growth plan (PGP)? I first heard this message as a young manager early in my career. It is a set of goals and objectives, and an action plan to help guide us each day. I am grateful that I was surrounded by so many great leaders who invested in me and showed me how to be intentional in my growth. Many have shared audio tapes for me to listen to - which are podcasts today. Many have taken me to leadership conferences to learn - which can now be seen on YouTube. Others have referred me to leadership books from which I experienced growth in all areas of my life - personal, professional, financial, family, spiritual, and community. I love talking about personal growth because it has helped me and can help others too. Some of my favorite conversations have included this topic.

In Episode 57, VP of the Employee Experience, Erica Rooney, shared how they use PGPs in their employee development. It's part of their DNA! I also talked with Vice President of Human Resources, LaToya Whatley, in Episode 35 about the importance of helping team members set goals to help them grow in their role. However, it starts with us. In fact, I remember when her daughter asked her, "Why are you always in school?" Latoya replied, "I'm always learning." Now *that* is living life in the leadership lane!

Industry certifications are also great to include in your personal growth plans. I remember getting my first certification in business. It was a CMC (Certified Moving Consultant) for household goods moving services. I remember being excited to pass the certification and add the acronym on my business card. Later, I earned my CRP (Certified Relocation Professional) from WorldwideERC, followed by HR certifications from HRCI and SHRM.

Someone on LinkedIn once sent me the following message: "I just noticed that you received a few certifications in the HR field. What motivates you for that?" As we corresponded, I learned the person was thinking about getting a certification and wanted perspective. I shared that it isn't as much about getting the certification as it is about the person you become as you go through the process. Earning different certifications have continued to play a role in my growth plans as a leader. They help not only with gaining knowledge, but also with building confidence!

John Maxwell has been a favorite mentor of mine for many years. He has been known to share in many teachings about how his dad used to pay him money to read books and share his takeaways in a book summary. What a great mentor his father was for him! John shares the "law of intentionality" in one of his books, *The 21 Irrefutable Laws of Leadership.* I recently heard him sharing a "highlight" of this chapter on his weekly podcast called "Minute with Maxwell." During the episode, he shared ways to create a personal growth plan. It's a great list to get us started!

1. Make a commitment to intentionally grow.
2. Make it public. Share it with those closest to you.
3. Identify 2-5 areas of growth. Areas of choice (attitude) and areas of skill (Speaking)
4. Invest an hour a day, every day. Preparation, Practice, Reflection.
5. Share your growth with those who are excited for you.

The key to PGPs is a commitment to *intentional* growth with a purpose to become better every day, so we can be in a position to help others in our path do the same.

Do you have a personal growth plan? How often do you review it? Have you shared it with others? If not, invest some time to create your PGP today... and make everyday a growth day!

I Felt Like Quitting

As mentioned previously, a few years ago I decided to start using the C25K app to develop a running routine. If you are looking to start running, I highly recommend it! The program starts out *easy walk / easy jog* in small time increments to help the runner get started and increases time/distance each week. The goal is to be able to run 3.1 miles (5K) and beyond without stopping on a regular basis.

When I started week four, the runs got much longer and the rest times were shorter. But on one particular day, I felt like I was running uphill into the wind with concrete shoes. Now don't get me wrong, I had run several 5Ks in the past, as well as competed in a 10-mile "tough mudder" event, but this particular day was HARD. On this day, it felt like I was trying to do life by myself.

So, what kept me going? In the app, there is a virtual coach that tells you when to stop and start. This "coach" has helped me stay on track, and it helped me get past the finish line that day. I felt like I had a friend there with me, pushing me to keep going and get better. I also had an accountability partner, motivating me stay on track! As I think about the times that I felt like giving up, I can consistently point back to one thing that has helped me to keep going - people around me!

I remember the challenges of going back to college with 2 small children while working a full-time job. I remember many times of struggling in my job, early in my career. I remember struggling at networking events trying to meet new people.

As I was running that day and during these challenging times in life, I thought back to something Jesse Itzler wrote in his book *Living with a Seal*. When he was getting tired during his run, he would say to himself, "Remember tomorrow." It would remind him of the story that he would tell himself the next day - did he quit, or did he finish?

So what story are you going to tell yourself tomorrow?

You see, this is leadership! It starts with leading ourselves, holding ourselves accountable when times get tough, and surrounding ourselves with people to cheer on, and who cheer us on. Most importantly, it's about people, and it will always be about people.

When we try to do life alone, we feel the struggle even more. When we walk with others, we feel a sense of togetherness and inspiration to get through the tough times – and we have someone to talk to along the way. This is the lane of fulfillment in life. It's all about the people!

So today, let's stay focused on what's most important - people! The people in your life who help you get through another week when the world gets tough. Your network, customers, co-workers, business partners, and friends who help you push through those days and keep going.

Some days are bigger than others, and some days are harder than others. Doing life together not only helps us get through those times, but also creates more opportunities of togetherness in our stories! So, keep going...the best is yet to come!

Goal-Focused vs. Growth-Focused

As we conclude this section, I want to share the importance of being growth-focused. Goals are important as they help us navigate, but having a growth focus is significant.

The list below is from my notes listening to *John Maxwell Leadership Podcast*. It was really impactful to hear this perspective and reflect on the power of growth. It's why growth day is every day!

Goal-Focused:
- Goals focus on the destination.
- Goals are seasonal.
- Goals challenge us.
- When we reach our goal – we often plateau.

Growth-Focused:
- People focus on the journey. (See the big picture.)
- Growth isn't seasonal – it's lifelong.
- Growth doesn't challenge people – growth changes people.
- When we reach a goal – we keep growing.

When we grow, we continually change. When we grow, we inspire. When we inspire, others grow!

How are you growing in your career? My sister Deanna once shared a cartoon picture of a squirrel in a tree and instead of the squirrel gathering nuts or food, he was gathering books. The quote on the picture reads, "Winter is coming." It's now framed in my office and reminds me of the importance of developing every day - because challenges and opportunities are just around the corner and we need to be ready.

Winter is coming…so start gathering resources, start gathering connections. It's not just about getting ready, it's about being ready!

What's Your Take?

What are you doing to grow as a leader? Are you growing with purpose? When is the last time you did something for the first time? Find a conference, a group, a certification or a learning module to sign up for and get started. As my mom Martha said in Episode 36, "It's not the product, it's the finished product that matters the most." Get Growing!

You're on the Air

It's Growth Day

Speak Your Influence

Build Your Brand

Building Community Networks

Turn It Up

Showing up with Gratitude

Recording with Purpose

Mic Up with Belief

Five Star Advice

Take the Challenge

CHAPTER 3

Speak Your Influence

"Don't let rejection tell you that you're not great!"
Camille Tate

I have enjoyed speaking for several years. I remember being so nervous in college when I was asked to give a presentation in communications class. I thought I was going to pass out in front of the class. Then later, I was asked to give my personal testimony at church. I was so excited and ready - until my name was called to come up and share. As I stood up, I felt numbness go through my legs and I wasn't sure how I was going to walk... I was so nervous! However, I have learned that the more I have spoken, the more confidence I have gained throughout my career.

In 2005, I joined a Toastmasters International Club in Dallas to work on my skills and I continued to learn from great speakers. However, the one area where I was stuck was choosing topics. I like to speak, but unless the audience needs to hear the message, it just doesn't feel right. For example, when I joined my company, I spoke a lot about relocation and ways to avoid problems that many people experienced. It was what I knew and wanted to share. I would speak to anyone who wanted to hear about it. However, if you are not in the relocating business or responsible for moving candidates, relocation probably isn't a topic you are interested in. People want to hear about ideas that can either help them where they are or inspire them to action.

In *Find Your Lane*, I shared a story about speaking at a conference and only having two people show up in my session. The conference included several breakout sessions and only two people showed up for my session about strategies to help employees relocate. I asked them if they wanted to move to another room and they said no, that they wanted to hear what I had to say. So, I delivered a one-hour presentation to 2 people. They loved it... and they needed the message.

When we speak, it's not about us, it's about them. When we speak, it's not about who is not there, it's about who showed up. Don't ever look at the empty seats. *Keep your eyes on the seats that are full.* We all have a lot more to share than we realize. We just need to go through the reflection process to think about what we know and what topics energize us so much that we feel like we need to share them with others.

I remember listening to Jennifer McClure, CEO of Unbridled Talent, on *Impact Makers* podcast one day during my drive to work. She was talking about speaking and I wondered if she might be able to help me. She is a keynote speaker and always draws a crowd at the national SHRM conference. I wasn't exactly sure how she could help, but I felt led to explore the possibility. So I reached out to ask for some advice. It was a call that helped change my perspective around speaking and really helped me think about other possibilities in my career. In fact, she recorded the conversation and later shared it as a podcast episode to help others who might have had some of the same questions that I had asked.

In our conversation, we talked about speaking topics, preparation and delivery, and generally all things speaking. It was energizing and inspiring. She shared some great advice. She said that since I was a sales leader with a network filled with HR professionals, and typically presented at HR conferences, perhaps I should consider talking about ways to help HR with selling their ideas to the C-suite. Now t*hat* was a topic that could really drive value for my audience. So I went to work on a presentation around selling to get more buy-in from the C-suite. I have delivered this presentation many times since then. It has become very popular, and it was one of the highest attended sessions at the 2020 HRSouthwest Conference. Hundreds of people showed up!

Since then, I have had conversations with many HR leaders about the importance of what I call "diamond influencers." This is a process we must all achieve in order to drive more influence in the workplace. Using the diamond-shaped diagram, I share that we need to start at the top with trust, and then move to the other corners of the diamond - finding a problem, building a business case, and developing sponsors to help sell the idea. When we achieve this, we can influence the process which explains the "I" in the middle of the diamond. I will share more below.

One of my favorite conversations was with Chief People Officer Diane Sanford (Episode 20) when she shared how busy C-level leaders are and how everyone is always asking for five minutes of their time. She shared some great ideas for us to develop more influence with top level leaders, such as respecting their time, being concise, beginning with the end in mind, and clarifying up front what you want to get out of the meeting.

> *Influence is about relationship-building, and that starts with Trust.*

You see, we are ALL in HR, we are ALL in customer service and we are ALL in sales! Influence is about relationship-building, and that starts with Trust. If we try to skip this step, we have a hard time getting buy-in from anyone. In this section, we are going to explore these points and how we can develop more influence in any role.

Getting to Buy-In

Have you ever struggled with getting buy-in for change in the workplace? I think many of us have in one way or another, from wanting to change to a new copier to work policy to organizational design. We often want things to change, but struggle to get leadership buy-in for various reasons. It could be too risky, too pricey, or out of alignment with business goals. Perhaps leadership doesn't think it's that big of a problem. Or maybe we just need to use a different approach to get buy-in from the top.

I once heard a story about a lady who worked for two different leaders, one of them was the outgoing leader, and the other was an incoming leader that she had previously worked with during her career. Someone in the organization heard that she had worked for the new leader and wanted to hear this lady's comparison to the outgoing leader. She said that the outgoing leader was *interesting*, but the incoming leader was *interested*. Did you catch that? The incoming leader was a relationship-builder and valued people by showing a genuine interest in others. In order to develop trust, we have to be willing to invest time to build relationships. No relationships, no trust. Let's look at this approach from a sales perspective:

Step 1: Build Trust. Trust is the foundation of leadership. It's the starting point for influence. Skip this step and you will face more challenges in your career and in life. One of my colleagues always talked about the importance of connecting with two up and two across in any organization. Getting to know leaders is critical to building trust. We can do this by listening and being interested in what is important to others. If you are new in the organization, it may take some time…so be patient.

Step 2: Find the "Right" Problem. Listen…if we're chasing the wrong problem, we are wasting our time. Sometimes, it might seem like there's a problem to us, but not to our leadership team. How big of a problem is it? What is it costing the business? Have you talked with others about it and asked for their perspectives?

One of the ways we can find a problem is to track questions that are being asked of us. When we hear the same question more than once, we need to write it down and discuss it with others to see if it's a problem in the organization. If you get the same question often, there are likely others who have the same question. Start keeping a list of questions or comments you hear on a daily basis and see what comes to the surface as potential problems.

Step 3: Build a Business Case. When you see multiple questions about the same issues, it's time to consider developing a business case. Many HR professionals miss the mark with this, because it takes time and effort. When we want change, we need to demonstrate why and how it will improve business results. The more the change is going to cost, the more research we are going to need to provide leaders in order to get them to consider the change. The business case needs to include stories, benchmarking, trends, and insights from other employees. Of course, it should also include options and recommended solutions.

Step 4: Develop Sponsors. Sponsors are like mentors, but they have great influence in the organization. When someone decides to make a change, it's important to show the value it will bring for the company. This is when we need to find others on our team who share the same perspective, which often means verifying team members' buy-in before presenting to decision makers. This is what we call a sponsor. I once heard one of our sales leaders in our company talk about the importance of having sponsors both across and up and down within the organization. When we have sponsors up and down, we have more perspectives and more buy in. Most importantly, if one of your sponsors leaves, then you still have other sponsors to help influence the process!

Step 5: Be Persistent. One of the things I learned early in my career was that NO could mean "not yet" or that not enough value was provided to warrant a conversation or make the change. And that's okay. We then have to determine what is the *real* reason for not changing, using a series of questions. Once we understand the *real* reason, we can then ask, "Do I need to find more value, or move on to something bigger?" The important thing to know is that it typically takes multiple calls or meetings to get to "yes" in sales, and most people give up after the first call. Persistence is more about how much we believe in the change…and how hard are we willing to work for it!

Let's take a closer look at each of these areas and how we can develop more influence in our workplaces.

1. Build Trust

How do you build trust in the workplace? It's a question I have asked many guests including CHRO Jill Cole (Episode 45). She replied, "It starts with doing what you are saying you are going to do!" As we talk about getting more buy-in and developing influence in the workplace, we must begin here. Trust is both horizontal and vertical. It takes a long time to build and a short time to destroy. So why do so many people skip this step? It's simple. Trust is all about building relationships and that takes time.

Lou Hotlz once said, "People ask themselves three questions when they meet someone new.

1. Can I trust you?
2. Are you committed?
3. Do you care?

Did you see what the first question was? Read it again... Can I trust you? It's *critical*! So how can we build more trust in the workplace?

Here are some examples you might consider:

Building trust comes from *developing relationships*. A great way to connect is to remember names, birthdays, and special events. This lets people know you are thinking about them and more importantly, that you care! My friend Yvonne Freeman sent me a text one day with a copy of an article about writing gratitude letters. She knew that I enjoyed writing these letters and that I might enjoy another perspective. This was another layer to the foundation of trust we have built for many years. It told me she was saying, "Hey, I'm thinking about you today and I think you might like this article or it might add value on your journey." She wasn't trying to *sell* to me...she was trying to *serve* me!

Don't just connect, build! How many connections do you have on LinkedIn or social media that you don't even know? Yeah...me too. We all do! We all like to connect, but we don't take time to build! Invest in the building!

Learn business acumen. This is about being quick to understand the situation in order to make decisions. Business acumen leads to better financial performance. This reminds me about a time when I took a study course for my HR certification, and our instructor, Barbara Hoover, said the most important thing we can do in any role is to "know the business." It's why we are here!

Here are some of the tips I have learned from high performers about building trust:

- Listen, relate, understand and listen more.
- Raise your hand to be involved outside of HR. Become a business partner!
- Make yourself the "go-to" person in the organization.
- Do what you say and say what you do.
- Communicate with excellence. Anticipate and push information, versus being pulled.
- Be consistent in your everyday leadership.

Building trust is about building a brand that says *I am going to do what I said I was going to do*. It's about raising your hand to learn more outside of your expertise. There are opportunities every day to build, but we must invest the time and not be so quick to move to the next step!

2. Find the "Right" Problem

Have you ever tried pushing a rope? You're right, no value there…but pulling a rope involves contribution and support. I remember as a young leader when I shared ideas with others, I got frustrated because nothing happened with them, only to realize that they may have been good ideas that just didn't align with the mission or goals of the company. I may have identified a problem, but it wasn't the *right* problem. Leaders don't have time to work on problems that don't align with company goals and objectives.

As leaders, we need to make sure we understand not just problems in general, but the right problems – the ones having the most impact on the organization. You see, every organization has problems, but the *right* problem gets attention and moves the needle of influence for us in any role. This goes back to knowing the business. Find the problems that create the most impact when solved, and you will have the leaders' attention and more influence. So how do we find the right problems?

Ask for a 15-minute meeting with the leader in the organization. "Be prepared," says Chief People Officer Diane Sanford (Episode 20). Leaders are busy and they need you to be clear and to-the-point on what problem you can solve.

Ask some of these questions:

- What are the challenges you are facing today?
- Why is this important to you?
- What do you have in place for this now?
- How does this impact your financial goals?
- How can I better serve you and your departments?
- What is this costing us and more importantly, what is this costing us *not to change*?
- Focus on one item at a time. What drives the biggest impact?

- Keep a question log and discuss topics that come up multiple times.
- Share brief stories when appropriate, around something you have experienced or where you have noticed opportunities for improvement.

3. Build a Business Case

Now that we have identified the problem, it's time to build a business case. It's all about anticipating the questions and finding the data. No data equals no influence. For example, when developing a leadership program, the first questions might be around costs for an in-house versus an outsourced program. My friend Suzanne Myers, Vice President of Human Resources (Episode 41) says, "It's the easy, hard stuff."

Have you ever seen the movie, *Jerry McGuire*? It's one of my favorites. In one scene, Rod Tidwell (played by Cuba Gooding, Jr.) wants his agent Jerry McGuire (played by Tom Cruise) to just "show him the money." It's such a great scene as he turns up the volume on his boom box and dances with a smile after saying, "Show me the money!"

In business, sometimes the ROI is tangible – a clear, easy-to-measure return on an investment – and sometimes it's more intangible, such as a better onboarding experience that drives retention and ultimately increases profits. See, we've already built trust with the leader, and we have found the right problems to solve. Now how can we build a business case that includes the data for change?

Here are a few ideas to consider:

- Do the work – research.
- Understand the "what" and the "why."
- Have the data – incorporate metrics.
- Know the market, keep it tight and compare it to industry.
- Use drip campaigns to share small messages over time.
- Speak the language of the business.
- Engage by challenging.
- Focus on one issue.
- Tell the time - don't try to tell how to build the clock.
- Share a story - help them see where this will take them.

4. Develop Sponsors

CEO David Windley (Episode 7) shared that mentors are good and can help with what you need to do, but sponsors can help you get to where you want to go. Do you have a sponsor in the workplace or in your volunteer community? Do you sponsor others? Maybe it's using a "2 by 2" approach, connecting with sponsors across as well as vertically in the organization, to gain a broader perspective and to help with buy in. The more sponsors, the more they can help you influence the process.

I once had a CEO reach out and ask me to mentor him in the networking space in an organization that I served. He wanted me to introduce him to some connections, and help him to partner with the right people for his business. Of course, I agreed, and was honored to help. He mentioned that his employee had asked why he would do this. In this employee's opinion, the President shouldn't need any help connecting with others. His response blew me away. He said, "This is true, but when you have a sponsor, they can help you skip steps, which saves a lot of time. Instead of showing up to several meetings, trying to meet people and connect, you show up to each meeting, a sponsor introduces you to several people for follow up, and you are immediately a credible person." Now *that* is sponsorship!

I have had some great sponsors during my career. They include family, friends, customers, business partners, and colleagues! I have found that when developing sponsors, it's important to remember the Dale Carnegie teaching, WIIFM – *What's in It for Me*? Sponsors enjoy helping those who have a hunger to grow in their leadership. Diane Sanford (Episode 20) pointed out that sponsors are sometimes the people who challenge and disagree. This is why it's important before sharing an idea, to reach out and ask your sponsors to poke holes in them, so that you are more prepared for any objections that might occur in the board room.

Here are some ideas for developing sponsors in your organization...

- Have meetings before the meeting.
- Serve others.
- Use the 100/0 rule.
- BE VIP (**V**isible, **I**n the moment, and **P**redictable).

- Connect 2 x 2 (know sponsors vertically and horizontally).
- Remember WIIFM.
- Use "relationshiping" - another word for networking - branded by my friend Seth McColley (Episode 5).

5. Be Persistent

It's hard to connect with people we don't know. In fact, I once read that a salesperson will often call an average of eight times before finally reaching someone. But in the world of connecting, it is much quicker when we have developed trust with someone or when we have sponsors who can introduce us.

I once met a friend for coffee and we were talking about her upcoming career change. As we finished, we were reminiscing about old jobs and I discovered that she had worked at a company I had been trying to reach out to for over 10 years. Unfortunately, I didn't know anyone and was unsuccessful in trying to connect. When I mentioned this, she said. "Hey, I know a lady in HR that I can connect you with. If you call her, let her know I referred you." Two weeks later, I was sitting across the table from this amazing lady, having a conversation. Two years later, we were doing business together and have since developed a friendship for life! You see, sponsors can help us connect with others. Then when we believe that we have something of value to offer our new connections, we will want to stay in the game of persistency to help them!

Have you ever felt like no one was listening and you were just ready to give up? We all have. Here are a few thoughts to inspire us to stay persistent.

- It takes an average of 8 calls to reach a prospect.
- Receiving a response of "No" may simply mean they don't have enough information to invest time in a discussion.
- Keep using drip campaigns to get traction and create momentum.
- Remember the "7 times 7" rule. In marketing it often takes presenting seven times before someone sees or hears the message to take action.
- If you really believe, you will look for a different way.
- Be tenacious, be tranquil and be consistent.

- Use the "feel, felt, found" method to handle objections: *I understand how you feel, others have felt the same way, but here is what I - or we - have found.*
- Sometimes a small win will lead to a big win.
- Don't give up. Never ever give up.

10 Common Threads

As I review these strategies, I notice there are several common threads to developing influence in the workplace. By applying them, we can have success in any role.

1. Don't rush the influencing process.
2. Layer ideas over time.
3. Socialize the heck out of your ideas.
4. Listen. Understand. Relate.
5. Have meetings before meetings.
6. Focus on WIIFM.
7. Be persistent.
8. Track it – Use the "3 question" approach.
9. Don't ever look at the empty seats.
10. Believe.

Speak with Confidence

When I joined Armstrong Relocation as a sales professional, I knew that in order to be effective, I needed to communicate well. So I joined a Toastmasters International Club in Irving, Texas. I knew this was important, so I committed to making it a priority every week. In order to have more, I needed to become more. So every Thursday at lunch, I drove to the local business and met with 10-12 people who all had the same goal, to be a more competent communicator.

I set a goal to receive a certificate. Achieving the certificate consisted of giving 10 presentations, starting with an easy 2- to 3-minute speech called an icebreaker, and leading up to a longer speech that incorporated things we learned during the course without using note cards. I remember there were days that I didn't feel like going, but I went anyway. There were times I did well and felt more confident, and days when I bombed and felt less confident. Speaking is an area in which leaders can make real impact, but it requires investing time to practice.

One of the exercises in Toastmasters was "word of the day," in which we tried to use the word in a sentence during the meeting and then during the week. I liked this exercise and learned a lot by doing it. It was not just about learning the word…it was also about being more aware of ways to speak with confidence. Words are important! Here are a few suggestions to think about the next time you find yourself sharing ideas or presenting a business case.

- I often hear people start with *honestly* and think…*Do people think you are not honest?*
- *Agreement* sounds so much better than *contract*!
- *Challenges* are much better than *problems*.
- I love future customer or future member, instead of prospect.
- Want to learn more? Check out 25 Words to Avoid in Sales at https://www.newbreedrevenue.com/blog/words-to-avoid-in-your-sales-pitch

The Secret to Influence
Building partnerships need to be part of our everyday in order for us to develop influence in the workplace and in our community, but it takes time and technique. Reflecting on my partnerships, I shared the following thoughts on social media:

It's like and love, trust and commitment.

It's the belief, values, and respect with conviction.

It's not the *some* days, but the *every* day.

It's investing in the building…

A partnership, a relationship, and companionship between two.

It's patience, frustration and annoyance too.

It's Sooner Magic and faith to help us through the tough times.

It's deep gratitude in reflection,

Of the imperfections that shape our perfections over time.

It's the easy, and the hard,

And the return is worth it all!

Bring Your Ideas

Want to develop more influence and lead with purpose? Always look for ideas to share with others. As I watched American actor and filmmaker, Tom Hanks, accept his award, I paid close attention to his comments. He shared three things every actor should do when they show up to the set or at the workplace. I vividly remember hearing the one thing that caught my attention and stuck with me ever since. He shared how important it was for people to "bring ideas" to the movie set or to the workplace. You see, we are always learning from others, which is how we get better in our careers and in our organizations. Ideas energize us, inspire us, and give us hope.

Bringing ideas also helps us with belonging and validation! One of the things I have enjoyed most about the *Life in the Leadership Lane* podcast is hearing ideas from each guest and sharing them with all of the listeners. This is why I say it's more than a podcast. In fact, Kelvin Goss, (Episode 14) says it's like a good vitamin that keeps us invigorated all day!

Look for the Lead Stories Each Day

In his book *Essentialism*, Greg McKeown shares a story about Nora Ephron, a famous screenwriter known for movies such as "Sleepless in Seattle" and "When Harry Met Sally." She remembered an assignment in high school, when the teacher asked students to look for a lead story, as it will contain the why, what, and when. The teacher shared the facts: "The principal and faculty will be traveling to Sacramento on Thursday for some training with some very well-known speakers. They will include an anthropologist, a college president, and the governor."

Everyone submitted different lead stories around each speaker...but they were all wrong. The lead story was "There will be no school on Thursday!" It's about looking for the problem, or what's missing, to help others see from a different angle!

Lastly, and most importantly... we must be present when sharing ideas or connecting with others. Being present in the moment is critical to

> ***Being present in the moment is critical to having the most impact.***

having the most impact. It tells them *you're important* and that you value the time and connection with them. In fact, this was my "Word of the Year" a few years ago. This takes practice and intentionality.

So how can we be more present? Start by slowing down, walking slowly through the crowd, holding a firm handshake for a second longer, or pausing to ask or answer questions. In Episode 61, Associate Professor and Author Dr. Derek Crews shared, "Engagement can be as simple as remembering someone's name." He added to make sure you look them in the eyes while speaking, for the deepest connection.

One thing we have all learned is that we can multitask such as walk and talk, or write down notes while listening, but what we can't do is multi-focus. We can't look at our phones while trying to make eye contact. Be *present* in your every day!

Where do you find ideas? What resources do you use in your daily practice - books, podcasts, conversations? Start making idea-sharing part of your everyday, and move leaders to inspire and change the workplace together!

In summary, there are 5 steps we must go through to develop more influence in the workplace.

1. Build trust
2. Find the right problem
3. Build a business case
4. Develop sponsors
5. Be persistent

If we try to skip steps, we will find challenges in every role. Trust the process and you will develop influence and move leaders to inspire and change the workplace every day!

What's Your Take?

What do you do to build influence? How can you start building influence in the workplace? Take the time to write down these 5 steps and post them on your wall as a reminder. Post them on social media to help others, too. Now, where can we start building relationships and trust in the workplace?

You're on the Air

It's Growth Day

Speak Your Influence

Build Your Brand

Building Community Networks

Turn It Up

Showing up with Gratitude

Recording with Purpose

Mic Up with Belief

Five Star Advice

Take the Challenge

CHAPTER 4

Build Your Brand

"Simply say, thank you."
Jamie Son

According to Lianne Daues, Talent Acquisition Leader (Episode 47), "Employer branding is one of those things that people don't really think about until they are in a recruiting or talent acquisition role and see how huge it is for organizations." She added that we need to be connecting and engaging with potential candidates at every point in the process. This employer brand is different than the company's overall brand and our personal brand!

Several years ago, when delivering a presentation, I asked the audience about the importance of branding. "We certainly know about employer branding, whether we realize it or not. I mean, who is not afraid to be in a long drive-thru line at Chick-Fil-A?" All hands went up, because we all know the line is going to move quickly, the food is going to be hot, and the hostess is going to respond to our "thank you" with, "It's my pleasure!" It's like this almost every time.

What about other brands? UnderArmor, Harley Davidson, Southwest Airlines, Nike, BMW, Apple…they all conjure up quality images, credibility and positive feelings because of their reputations. Company branding is important because it provides a memorable impression and reminds customers of the experience they can expect from the company. It's a differentiator from the competition.

People like knowing what they are going to experience. In Episode 39, Kim Zoller, CEO, shared the importance of branding in her experience with the store Lululemon. She always knows what she's going to get and it doesn't matter who she is working with. They are all there to serve.

Our personal brand is our character and what people think about us when we are not around.

So, we know about an employer brand, but what about the employee brand? That's right, WE all wear a brand too. Our personal brand is our character and what people think about us when we are not around. Think about the person sitting in your reception area answering the phones. What words come to mind? For our receptionist, I think of the words pleasant and dependable. When I walk in the door of our office, I know I'm going to receive a pleasant greeting every time. *Every time!* When our guests walk in the door, they are also greeted with a pleasant "Hello" or "Welcome," and "May I help you?" If I need support on a project and I ask for help, I know it will get done – with excellence! You see, we all have brands and it's so important that we are aware of who we are and how we are perceived in the workplace. So, what's your brand? Are you dependable, trustworthy, honest, consistent, kind, friendly, genuine, authentic or approachable?

While I was speaking with Kim, she also suggested that we think about the last five people we were with yesterday. We are constantly thinking about and making decisions such as: *Do we like them? Do we trust them? Do we want to work with them?* It's all based on how we feel, and how we feel is based on their consistency. Personal branding is more important than ever today because of the competition and social media. We all have the opportunity to build a great brand just like employer brands, but it needs to start with self-awareness.

Building Self-Awareness

Do you know who you are? What about who others think you are? When these are in alignment, you are on your way to living a brand with purpose.

Self-assessments are a great way to start. They provide insight to help us identify values, fears, motives, and more. Just a few options for self-assessment include DISC, Myers Briggs Type Indicator, Predictive Index and StrengthsFinder 2.0. But I would like to share a real-world branding exercise that I learned from my friend Jennifer McClure in an *Impact Makers* podcast. This exercise is a great tool to help us identify our brand, but it takes some vulnerability.

To get started, reach out to your network of friends, family, business partners, etc. Ask them to share three words they think of, when they think of you…when you are not in the room. You can actually post the question on social media. Leave it up for about a week, then take the words and put them into a word art to see what words populate. Make sure to include multiples of the same word when repeated, because the more the same word is entered, the bigger the word gets in word art. When I decided to do this, I posted the question on Facebook, LinkedIn, Twitter and Instagram. I received the most responses from Facebook, followed by LinkedIn, with a few on Twitter and Instagram. When I finished, I copied the words to a word document from all four sites, then copied and pasted everything to wordart.com. Some of my results included Authentic, Committed, Caring, Driven, and Relocation. These results represent how I show up every day, both offline and online. Once you post and get your results, then you get to decide if this is the brand you want. If you do, keep pushing and living this brand. If not, then choose to change.

I had a friend who shared with me that his brand was "Bold," and asked what I thought. I said it was quite inspirational - people probably look at him as being bold because he shares a lot of content on video and it is inspiring to those in his network. If you have a brand of "great cook," you probably post a lot about cooking or food. But what if you want to change that brand? You can! Just start posting and talking about other things, and it will change over time. The key to building your brand is consistency. You have to live it *everywhere* - at work, volunteering, and in your home. Build a brand that says, "Hey, you can count on me for this!"

Brand Building

One thing that stands out when interviewing high performers is the work they have put in to not only achieve success in their career, but also in their brand. I know this because when I share information about a guest that I have interviewed, many people will comment, "He/she is amazing," or "I can't wait to hear this episode," or "This guest is the best leader I know." During the show, as their story unfolds, they all have common threads that have ultimately shaped their brand.

Here are four things we all should consider when building a brand:

1. Start with who. All of my guests talk about mentors who stood out in helping them find their lane. Who do you want to be? Make sure to align with who you are.

2. Start where you are. When my guests share their stories, they all started in different places. Some early in their career, others much later.

3. Write down goals that include steps for building your brand. Be intentional.

4. Show up, be consistent, be engaged, and be YOU.

When I was interviewing Senior HR Business partner Justin Dorsey in Episode 64, he shared his thoughts about shaping our brand. The first thing he mentioned is that he wants to be known for the same guy at work, at a networking event, at college football games, in the community and in his home. He doesn't want to be the guy speaking while someone in the crowd is saying, "*That's not who he is.*" In other words, he wants to make sure he has a brand of authenticity. This resonated with me so much. I have worked hard to be the same person everywhere. I once heard the late Tony Hsieh, author of *Delivering Happiness,* and his perspective around work-life balance. He said that it's not about work-life balance, but about work-life *integration.* Are you trying to be someone different at work than you are when you leave?

I remember when I first started engaging in social media and I was trying to decide if I should connect with people I work with, or customers, or others in the community. I found it difficult to decide because I never could put my finger on why I should or shouldn't connect with certain people or groups. I finally made the decision that I am me, and that's the only person I know how to be - at work, in the community and in my home. The audience and setting may differ, but we should all strive to be the same person no matter who is watching.

Later in our conversation, Justin shared a story about the movie, *Drive to Survive.* He said he wasn't necessarily a race car driver enthusiast, but he was fascinated by the guys in the pit crew who were part of the driver's success. He didn't say it, but what he was getting at was building a brand in any role. He shared that the guys who were changing the tires or checking the car were probably some very smart guys, some of them might even be great drivers. They probably didn't grow up to be in the pit crew, but if they are able to execute in that area and change that tire to the best of their ability, that's where they got noticed and were able to take on more responsibilities.

So, keep your eyes open because there may be some hidden talent on your team right now, changing tires. And if your job is to change tires right now, change them as fast and as well as you can! Answering the phones? Execute well. Trying to work your way up in your department? Fulfill your current responsibilities to the best of your ability. You are building a brand that will eventually get noticed!

Promoting Your Brand

Several years ago, I read about a Domino's pizza franchise in Russia that found a unique way to promote their company. They offered 100 pizzas for free for 100 years if customers would get a tattoo of their company logo and post it on social media with the hashtag #DominosForever. The promotion was supposed to run for 60 days, but they had to discontinue after just four days because so many people were participating. The company ended up with 381 people who qualified for the deal! Now *that's* branding!

Social media is such a great way to build a brand, but it's also a way to "kill" your brand. It takes years to build it up and much, much less time to knock it down. I have embraced social media since I started my first LinkedIn page in 2006, later building out Facebook and Twitter in 2009. There are so many opportunities to connect and promote your brand, but it takes time. When I started a YouTube account, it took several years to get 100 subscribers. Today, we have so many ways to build a brand.

Unfortunately, it is similar to working out. Many people will get on the bandwagon and try it, but if they don't see early results, they quit…or they quit being consistent. Building a brand takes time and discipline.

When I began my career with Armstrong Relocation, I decided to start writing a blog around relocation. I had been studying the industry for the past 2 decades. I thought people might be interested in reading some of the stories about families moving, to learn tips for making it a better experience. When I posted the first few articles, I heard a lot of…crickets! I wondered, *is anybody reading this? What else am I passionate about?* I love reading books about leadership and stories that inspire, so the next post, I wrote about a book and some of my key takeaways. It was energizing to see some of the feedback. I thought *this is it! I am going to write about both leadership and relocation.* Since then, I have added other topics that are meaningful to me, knowing that it may not help everyone, but it might help someone.

This is also a great way to promote your brand. Find what you are passionate about and start writing about it. Share it with your team in an email, in a blog, or on your social media sites. Share it in the workplace with other colleagues and ask for their perspectives.

Our Chief Customer Officer shares stories with us each week called "Friday Flash." It's a great way to share success stories or teaching moments with your team. Once you start gaining momentum, you will begin to experience people looking to you for advice on that subject. I remember once during an interview, hearing the interviewer say, "Since you are a leadership expert, let me ask…." As I heard those words, I thought, *Wow, I never thought about this while going through the process!* I had simply focused on reading and writing about leadership topics I enjoyed.

What brand are you promoting? Remember…we get to *choose* our brand, so make it count!

Living Your Brand Every Day
How do we know when our brand is strong? Think about brands such as Harley Davidson, a company with a following who paints their body

with wings, or Apple, with customers who get the Apple tattoo to show their affinity with the brand. While other brands pay people to get their tattoo, such as Domino's, or the Ohio-based restaurant MELT - which gives 25% off for the logo - others don't need incentives. *They live it!* They are proud to be part of the community, because it's something bigger than their career. If you build a brand with excellence, you may not get people to paint a picture of your face or your name on their bodies, but people may follow you and promote you to others. What will it take to build this brand? Let's take a look at a few ideas to "live your brand" with excellence every single day.

1. Read and study things that matter to you.
2. Identify your target audience.
3. Make sharing part of your everyday.
4. Engage in feedback.
5. Be consistent.

One of the biggest mistakes we make is to talk about things we don't care or know much about, just to get attention. You see, building a brand is all about who you are and what you believe. I typically write about things that energize me, things that I believe in. It is a reminder for me, and if it helps others then that's a bonus. When I write about ways to be a better leader, it's a reminder for me to use this strategy or process to be a better leader. When I write about strategies to relocate talent, it helps me with reflection and to look through the lens of my customers to understand how to serve them better. When I write about continuous improvement, such as tips to be a better speaker, or when I get a certification, it fills me with gratitude knowing how challenging it can be and how this might help others looking to skill up professionally!

Use Your Voice to Build Brand

Early in my career, I sat at the table with the sales leadership team right after I joined Armstrong Relocation, thinking, *How do these men and women know so much about a company, or how do they know how to solve so many problems?* I wondered how they had so much knowledge. Now, several years later, I see how this happens. It happens through our *experiences*. It happens when we have the courage to choose the pain of discomfort of change in order to get better. When we choose to go through the process of learning, we grow through our experiences. I remember early on, I wanted to learn from the ones who had the most experience, so I didn't always speak up. I wanted to be a sponge and learn from some of the best. And now that I am the older person in the room, I want to hear ideas from the younger generations. It is a paradigm shift. The point is, we can all add to the conversation. Speaking up - even if you don't feel like you know a lot - can help more than you think. It also helps you build a brand of someone who wants to continuously learn and grow in the company. We don't always see things from the same perspective, and we can learn in every stage of our career. This is also an opportunity to build a brand that says *I am all in for learning and bringing new ideas to help grow our company.*

Hey, You're a Natural!

I recently had the opportunity to present an "Ignite" presentation at our annual Texas Relocation Conference in Carrollton, Texas. It was called *The High Cost of a Low-Cost Move.* Ignite presentations are short, five-minute presentations that have 20 slides, with each slide transitioning to the next after 15 seconds. The idea is to share a relevant topic and give the audience a "sneak peek" or summary of an idea, to see if they have interest for a deeper dive or follow-up in the future. I love this presentation format, because it allows you to see as many as 10 different speakers within an hour timeframe. It is both educational and entertaining, seeing and hearing the speakers share their expertise and passion during the presentations. It is also very challenging as a speaker to stay on track with the timing. It takes a lot of practice to deliver the presentation within the timeframe and with excellence!

After I finished my presentation, an industry colleague congratulated me and said "Bruce, you're a natural!" It was such a kind thing to say, and I was very appreciative. Not to mention, it made me feel great! When I reflected on the comment, I was humbled as I remembered some of the times when I wasn't so much of a natural, and how I had worked to build a brand to be a better speaker.

I remembered…

- When I was required to give a speech as a freshman in college, I was so nervous I could hardly breathe.
- When I was asked to share my business plan in front of all of our management team, including the CEO, in my first real job after college.
- When I committed to giving my personal testimony at church. As the pastor asked me to come up to share, I thought I was going to fall down because my legs were trembling as I walked to the podium.
- When I decided to join Toastmasters so I could get better at communicating in my profession, and decided to participate in "table topics." During the meeting, I was given a topic and had one minute to share my thoughts. All I said was "um, um, um, um, um…" and then I sat down! It was a complete failure!
- When I published my first book, I was asked to speak. I held and looked at my notes during the entire presentation.

Have you ever experienced any of these moments? It's so much easier to look back and see what it took to get to success, than it is to look ahead to see what it will take to have success. This is the same for building a brand. I remember taking piano lessons for almost two years. Many times, I thought about giving it up because it was so difficult. It took time to practice. However, the more I practiced, the better I got. Every time I learned a new

> *It's so much easier to look back and see what it took to get to success, than it is to look ahead to see what it will take to have success.*

song, I progressed to a new level. It's challenging to become an expert or to master anything. In fact, Malcolm Gladwell shared in his book *Outliers* that the "10,000-Hour Rule" is the key to success in any field. This rule states that you can become successful at something by practicing that specific task 20 hours a week for 10 years. Wow – 10 years? That's a lot of practice!

Building a brand takes time and a lot of work. It's hard to put ourselves out there too…to be vulnerable and willing to let people know we are a work-in-progress. We want to be accepted and validated early and often. But it is when we are *challenged* that we experience real change!

In 2020, our CLIMB book club read *The Power of Moments* by Chip and Dan Heath. Each week, our group posted something from the book for others to comment on. One week, my friend Krystal Yates posted this excerpt: "To live a longer life, scare the hell out of yourself regularly. Everyone go out and do something scary this week." It's amazing how much we grow when we make the decision to get better in our role, or change a policy, or even a career. The only way to get better is to go through the process and experience life. It will take time. It will take practice. It will take failure. But most of all, it will take help from others. Once we've gone through the process, we may one day be "a natural" and in a position to share this knowledge with others looking to elevate their career and their life.

It takes vulnerability and community to go through the peaks and valleys of building a brand. In Episode 43, Melissa Goebel shares that we learn from the peaks and valleys. It may not feel like you are getting traction, but if you keep believing, keep going, and keep finding ways to drive your passion, one day you may be asked how you became such an expert in your field!

Back to Employer Branding

I once heard keynote speaker, Mike Singletary (NFL Hall of Fame) say, "Do you know what I enjoyed most about playing football? The opportunity to play." Likewise, I recently took advantage of the opportunity to speak at and attend TalentNet Live in Dallas, Texas. TalentNet Live is a conference that brings together some of the best of the best in Talent Acquisition to help attendees learn the latest in finding and attracting great talent for the workplace. The conference boasted a stellar group of speakers and fascinating titles such as *AI, Employer Branding, Today's War on Talent,* and *The Latest in Technology*. They also offered a "TA Improv" for attendees to participate as speakers. It was outstanding! I had so many takeaways, but I want to focus on one of the session insights that will help any company expand their employer brand…even with a limited budget.

The strategy session was "Employer Brand Versus Authentic Culture," facilitated by Jorgen Sundberg, CEO for Link Humans. The panelists represented huge companies such as Toyota, American Airlines, and Anthem. They shared perspectives for shifting language around new generation hiring, the biggest questions asked to find best talent, and the secret sauce to establishing brand recognition. During the session, Jorgen asked a question that really resonated with me. He asked the panelists for their perspective on how employers can get the "biggest bang for their buck" to expand their employer brand.

My takeaway: A better brand will help your company in so many ways, including attracting and retaining great talent to build a great company. The following are some of my notes and ideas to TRANSFORM your employer brand with a limited budget.

- Invest in your people. Spend time with your hiring managers and recruiters.
- Use social media to tell stories - not only what you do, but also why you do it.
- Use a company #HashTag to build a community. What's your company hashtag?
- Teach employees to be better networkers in their community.
- Find the people in the company who are passionate and partner with them.
- Ask your leaders to provide stories for employees to share with their networks.
- Engage your employees and ask for ideas to share with others.
- Invest time in an outreach for everyone to connect, and use company #hashtag.
- Be authentic. Everyone in the company is unique.
- All of us have an army. Invest the time and watch the transformation.

One of the quotes in my book *Find Your Lane* is, "The bigger the WHY, the easier the HOW," by Jim Rohn. A great strategy always starts with a goal, which is the "what" behind the "why." Do you have a great company brand? What do your employees say on social media, glass door, etc.? What can you do to expand your employer brand so others know about you and want to join your team? Now is a great time to meet with your people and start the brand recognition and transformation process. By being a person who is looking for ways to help the company, you will elevate your employee brand. When you find a way to apply that characteristic in your company, it will help your company elevate. It might be a SMALL that starts something really BIG!

So, what are the leadership brands that I have observed from guests on the *Life in the Leadership Lane* podcast?

My Top 10:

1. They show up.
2. They are confident.
3. They believe.
4. They learn from failure.
5. They are committed.
6. They are continuous learners.
7. They have mentors.
8. They know their purpose.
9. They know their values.
10. They serve others.

What stands out to you? I want to challenge you to choose one of the characteristics above and share it with your leadership team to start some dialogue.

Remember the word BRAND to start from where you are.

B Be Consistent!

R Relationships Matter!

A Authenticity Is Best!

N Network with a Purpose!

D Dream it, Do it!

What's Your Take?

Do you know your personal brand? Do you want to know? Now is a great time to try this exercise. Reach out to your network and ask them for three words that describe you. Have a conversation with your leadership team to learn how you can impact the employer brand...doing that will ultimately impact your personal brand.

You're on the Air

It's Growth Day

Speak Your Influence

Build Your Brand

Building Community Networks

Turn It Up

Showing up with Gratitude

Recording with Purpose

Mic Up with Belief

Five Star Advice

Take the Challenge

CHAPTER 5

Building Community Networks

*"I used to say yes to everything, and now I say
yes to things that make the biggest impact."*
Angela Shaw

One of the questions I asked President and CEO Bronwyn Allen on Episode 71 was around strategies she uses to grow her team members. When someone on her team asks about ways to grow and advance in the company, she often encourages her team members and others to go outside the workplace and find an association where they can serve as a volunteer leader. This is something a lot of people don't think about when it comes to growing our career. Volunteer leadership has so much value when it comes to education, networking and serving in the community. The conversations and connections we experience through volunteering help us become more not only as a volunteer leader, but also in our workplaces and in our homes. Are you involved in your community?

We all have an opportunity to volunteer in our community, but it takes courage to step up and opt in to the conversation. We can volunteer for little league, our local school, our community, or our industry association. Every organization is looking for volunteers. It doesn't require as much time as what you might imagine, but it does take a commitment to be all in.

I have always wanted to make an impact in my career. I just didn't know how as a young leader. We tend to think it has to be something extraordinary, when often it's the ordinary that makes an impact. I have enjoyed volunteering during my entire career. I have found that it has helped me grow my leadership in so many ways, but the most important has been through learning how to serve others. It also provides me with a place outside of the workplace to create friendships for life.

I once heard Sarah Blakely, CEO and Founder of SPANX, share, "The more we learn, the more we can help others." I love this perspective, and it can be used with anything - the more we grow, the more we can grow others. The more we connect, the more we can help others connect. The more opportunities we take to lead, the more opportunities we have to develop other leaders around us. This is where we find joy. This is where we find purpose in the workplace and in life. When we take the opportunity to develop others, we become extraordinary! Finding a place to volunteer in our community is definitely a way to grow as a leader.

In Episode 53, VPHR Lisa Collins said, *"I think anybody - no matter their position - can be a leader formally or informally."* We all have opportunities to develop others through our actions in modeling leadership. When I was younger, I got involved in my kids' sports as a coach. I coached my kids in t-ball and baseball. I also coached them in football. When they got older, I volunteered for the Quarterback Club in their high school. During that time, I learned from other coaches, and had the chance to develop kids in both sports and in life. When I look back, it was one of the most fulfilling experiences in my life.

When someone asks you to help, just say yes. Even better, go ask someone what you need to do to become a volunteer leader. This is a great way to get started. Ask anyone in a volunteer organization and they will tell you their story about how they got into a leadership role. Most of them just asked, and then kept showing up. When you do, you will not only develop your leadership, but you will also experience many opportunities to help develop others.

While leading DallasHR, an association that supports the human resources community in Dallas, Texas, I was asked to be part of a leadership development program called Leadership Links. It was a program to help volunteer leaders develop their skills to become better leaders for themselves, their volunteer organizations, and their workplaces. To develop the program, we held a lot of meetings over a year and a half. I knew it would take a lot of time when I committed to the design team, but I knew it would be worth it. Within the first 5 years, we developed almost 100 leaders who completed a 6-month training course during the year. At the end of each program, attendees shared testimonies filled with both laughter and tears of joy. Almost everyone said that they felt like they were now better leaders as a result of being part of the class. Attendees were more confident and looked forward to using their skills to help others. But the most common threads were that everyone expanded their network, and members of the group had become very close friends - it felt like a family. Since then, I have helped design a development program for Texas SHRM, an organization that supports SHRM chapter leaders in the human resources community across the state of Texas. I can't wait to continue watching these community networks flourish.

So, what are some ways we can grow our community network?

- Volunteer in an industry-specific organization.
- Start or join a book club.
- Listen to a weekly podcast with your team. (I know a good one to consider.) ☺
- Volunteer in your child's school.
- Engage in a social media community.
- Attend a learning conference with others to share the experience.
- Take an online course with a business partner.
- Sign up for Toastmasters to develop as a speaker in community.
- Start an online mastermind group.

The most important thing is to get involved. When we connect with community, it gives us more opportunity to learn and share perspectives and ultimately become better together.

The question that connected me to Hall of Fame Coach Bob Stoops

Many years ago, I heard John Maxwell talk about interviewing his childhood hero, John Wooden, the Hall of Fame basketball coach at UCLA. John talked about the time he invested as he prepared for the meeting, which included writing multiple pages of questions so that he could make the most use of Coach Wooden's time. He wanted to learn as much as he could from one of his favorite leaders. In an interview, John talked about how he connected with Coach Wooden during a networking event when he asked someone the question "Who do you know that I should know?" It's such a great question. He also described how Coach Wooden was like a well, filled with wisdom-of-life principles. It was inspiring.

I also interviewed one of my leadership heroes, Bob Stoops. I connected with him through a friend while networking after I asked the question "who is someone on your wish list that you would like to meet and interview one day?" When they turned the question back around to me, I shared that Bob Stoops, also a hall of fame coach, was on my wish list!

Coach Stoops became the head football coach at the University of Oklahoma during the late 90s, when I was a young manager experiencing a lot of challenges in the workplace. I remember the confidence that permeated from him as he spoke to the media, and how inspiring it was. Since then, he went on to become the all-time most winning college football coach at Oklahoma. Under his leadership, the OU Sooners won a national championship and 10 conference titles. A statue of him stands just outside the stadium, next to other legendary coaches.

During my interview with him, we talked about his book *No Excuses: The Making of a Head Coach* and some of the stories he shared in it about family, football, and leadership. Reflecting on my interview with Coach Stoops, here are some of the lessons I learned that had the most impacted on me the most during our visit. I hope you find value in them as well!

1. Surround yourself with great people. Coach Stoops played for his father Ron Sr. at Cardinal Mooney High School in Youngstown, Ohio. He went on to play for Hall of Fame coach Hayden Fry, and later coached with Hall of Fame coaches Barry Alverez, Hall of Fame coach Bill Snyder, and Hall of Fame coach Steve Spurrier, just to name a few. He was always surrounded by great men in his own program, and he continues to stay connected to great coaches and players! *Who are you surrounded by in your network?*

2. See the field (big picture). During the interview, Coach Stoops talked about how his dad taught him a lesson while watching game film in the kitchen as it projected onto the refrigerator. He said most people watch the ball during the play, but his dad taught him to "see the game." He was referring to how they would watch the same play over and over and over until they could see every angle. *What do you need to "see" in the workplace?*

3. Compartmentalize success. Don't be afraid to change it up each year. Coach Stoops took his players to the basketball court one week for some competition, to change up practice. He was animated as he shared stories about some of the big lineman dunking the basketball and shooting long-range jumpers. *What do you need to change up in your daily practices in the workplace?*

4. Make others feel important. When asked was about the importance of volunteering, he said that when he visited with kids at the OU Children's Hospital, it was important to make them feel important. Coach Stoops advocates for the HBC Champions Foundation to support local children's hospitals in the Norman and Oklahoma City area. *In what ways do you make others feel important?*

5. Have a purpose. During the end of the interview, Coach Stoops commented that he had found his purpose during his hospital visits. When you know your purpose, life is just different. It's intentional and choices are easier to make in our everyday. *What is your purpose?*

Coach Stoops also talked about the importance of recruiting for character, giving tough love, and pushing through tough times. It was a conversation I will never forget. Coach Stoops is full of wisdom - like John Maxwell shared about Coach Wooden - and I was so grateful to have had the opportunity to visit with him and hear his perspective. Many of us know these lessons, but it is essential to reflect on how we are doing in these areas in order to be better leaders. I am also excited to have the opportunity to share with others to help them become better leaders, too.

So, who do you know that I should know? It's time to ask the question during your next networking event!

CLIMB with Purpose

I remember it like it was yesterday. I was sitting in a room full of volunteer leaders following a fun day at the HRSouthwest Conference in Fort Worth, Texas. A small group of us were talking about different leadership books that we had recently finished, the energy we get from learning, and how we should start a book club. So, we decided to read a book and meet to discuss takeaways. The book we decided to start with was called *Dare to Lead* by Brene Brown. We purchased the book and met at a local restaurant to discuss what we learned and to get different perspectives about how to apply some of the lessons in the workplace.

I wanted to name the group, so I started playing with words and came up with CLIMB, which stood for **C**onnect, **L**ead, **I**nspire, **M**entor and **B**uild. I wanted the group to be more than a book club. I wanted it to be more like a leadership community – a group that had a purpose in our everyday leadership. Everything we did would align with Connecting, or Leading, or Inspiring, or Mentoring, or Building our career and our community! In 2019, I talked to the group about expanding online the following year, so that we could *CLIMB* with others around the world. We have read a book every other month and we've used social media to post and connect with others. Using the social media platform Facebook, we have posted thoughts on leadership, inspiring others, mentoring and coaching, and building community. It is now a group of more than 150 members and growing.

You see, we don't have to have a title - we just need to have a heart to serve! Creating community learning gives us a platform to learn and grow with others.

Extending the Play

As I was watching a college football, I noticed a common thread when coaches described quarterbacks who were making impact. They would emphasize the importance of "extending the play." This is when a quarterback doesn't have a receiver open, so he continues to move around and keep his eyes down the field. He may run, but he continues to look for an open receiver until the last minute. He plays with HEART!

Some of the best business leaders also "extend the play" - which helps them to create success.

On Episode 23, Global Talent Acquisition leader Annie Carolla talked about how some guests are able to go beyond the answer when being interviewed. They continue to share points and perspectives, sometimes including stories to bring the answer to life with energy and color. I mentioned that this is comparable to players who are able to "extend the play." These guests go above and beyond, always finding ways to creatively extend the answer when asked a question.

It's not about just continuing to talk and share perspective, but relating it with stories and insight. Yes, they have incredible experience, but their HEART is in everything they do. When we extend the play, we create stories, we challenge thinking, and more importantly we provide inspiration and belief.

What about when we respond to emails at work or engage in a social post related to our industry? Do we just answer the question, or do we "extend the play" by taking a few extra minutes to look up an email address or website link to add to the response? Do we write in the subject line before we hit reply or do we just respond and hit send? This is the difference between a good experience and an exceptional one. Exceptional leaders know how to "extend the play." They provide more information with easy access, they follow up, and they continue to find ways to create a better experience.

So how can we extend the play in our career?

One of the books we read in our CLIMB book club is called *The Heart of Leadership*. It is about a young manager, trying to learn to be a better leader. His mentor sent him to talk with others to find out how he could lead better in the workplace and in his home. The end of the story captured the 5 lessons he learned on his journey to be a better leader.

So, what are the lessons? I received the lessons below from my friend and Director of Human Resources, Amanda Perrydore. She captured this outline for our group, which helped us put everything in perspective. She not only captured the outline, but she "extended the play" by making a picture for others in the group to print off to put in a frame, as a reminder to play with HEART in the workplace and in our home! In fact, mine is framed in my home office to remind me of the moment.

Here is the outline:

1. **H**unger for wisdom…Your quest for wisdom is a hunger that will never be satisfied. Never stop learning. Seek counsel from others.
2. **E**xpect the best. True leaders see a better future. Leaders are dealers in hope. Hope for a better tomorrow.
3. **A**ccept responsibility. Look in the mirror when things don't go well and look at others with praise when they do.
4. **R**espond with courage. Take action to build courage. Leaders don't wait, they initiate.
5. **T**hink "others first." The most important characteristic because it reflects your heart. The best leaders serve.

As you can see, extending the play is a matter of **HEART**! When we play with heart, we can extend the play in every situation. Is your heart in your work, and everywhere you go? Find a way to extend the play and you will not only experience more, but you will become more in everything you do.

What's Your WHY?

I once read about Thomas Pierpont Langley, the man who set out in the 1900's to be the first man to pilot an airplane. Have you heard of him? Most of you probably haven't. But you have probably heard of Orville and Wilbur Wright. They were just a few hundred miles away, working on their own flying machine. Thomas Pierpont Langley was highly regarded and well-educated. He worked as a mathematics professor at Harvard and had numerous resources. The Wright brothers didn't have the resources and yet they were able to pull off the unthinkable, flying their first airplane on December 17, 1903. What was the difference? It was all about a cause. Thomas Pierpont Langley was looking to be the first, while the Wright brothers were looking to change the world. It was their WHY that created their success!

We recently read the book *Start with Why* by Simon Sinek in our CLIMB book club and there are many stories that have similar context. Martin Luther King said, "I have a dream" (not "I have a plan") to start a civil rights movement. President Kennedy shared his vision to put a man on the moon. You see, there are leaders, and there are those that lead. Those that lead inspire us every day.

> *When purpose and career align, life is just better.*

Who are you inspiring as a leader?
Guests on *Life in the Leadership Lane* inspire. They have a belief or cause! One of my favorite Ted Talks is "The Golden Circle" by Simon Sinek, in which he shares the importance of knowing your WHY and starting with WHY. He says, "People don't buy what you do, they buy why you do it." Go on YouTube and watch it. It is well worth the five minute investment.

Many times, we read articles, watch videos, and check off boxes, but we don't apply what we learn…we just keep moving. However, I believe you are reading this book for a reason and I want to challenge you to *stop and think about your why*. Write it down and share it with others. It's your purpose! When our purpose and career aligns, life is just better. We are more positive, we are more optimistic, we are more resourceful, we have more empathy, and we have more energy. It's one of the keys to success. When we believe, *really* believe in what we do, it makes an impact, makes us authentic, builds relationships and trust, and takes us to places we never dreamed.

Here is an example - my "why." In my company, I want to "move people to inspire and change the workplace." I do this with a commitment to continuous learning, so I can help others when relocating talent. I do this through connecting with people and resources - so I can help others connect with resources - and I use my books, blog, and podcast to share the message to inspire. It's my everyday "why!" In my volunteer role as a Texas SHRM Assistant State Director, my "why" is to help grow our board members and chapter leaders to help them to grow SHRM chapters in communities across the great state of Texas! Why? Because I believe it will change their workplaces and their lives! You see, when we help others grow, they will model leadership and as a result, they will bring positive change to their workplace!

In one of the exercises we completed in CLIMB, we wrote down our WHY or our purpose statements and shared it with other CLIMB members. It was a lot of fun seeing the different "why" statements in the group. We even posted them on social media for others to see. It was energizing! This is something you can do with your company, your department or your group. Ask everyone to write down why you work there, or why you volunteer, or why you belong to a certain group. Then collect the quotes and share. It creates engagement and belonging, and most importantly, you get to help each other grow!

What's your why? Write it down this week and share it with others in your community.

Community Motivates Us

It was a cold, windy morning as I started stretching for my morning workout. I really didn't feel like getting out of bed this morning, but I knew my son-in-law would be just on the other side of the door waiting for me to get started with our 5am workout. We had been working out every day for the past couple of months and had generated some great momentum in our health and wellness.

> *You see, life in the leadership lane isn't about the leader – it's about the journey and having the ability to influence others along the way!*

As I ran that morning, I thought about the times in my life when I had enjoyed success as a leader and had felt like I had made traction in my career. It was when I had included others on my journey. You see, life in the leadership lane isn't about the leader - it's about the journey and having the ability to influence others along the way! Some of my biggest moments have been when I was connected and growing with others. It was when my wife pushed me to finish college. It was when my dad asked me to lead the bowling proprietors' group. It was when my brother handed me an audio tape to help me with my leadership growth. It was when my boss handed me a book and challenged me to become more. It was in each of the conversations I have had with high-performing leaders on my podcast.

One of the questions I like to ask guests on *Life in the Leadership Lane* is around advice, purpose and gratitude. I have noticed there is a common theme among all of these leaders. They all talk about their teams and their people. Leadership is about doing work together - growing together, working together, and sharing experiences together. The best leaders know the importance of people and demonstrate this by connecting, challenging, and recognizing their potential.

I remember one afternoon when I decided to play an impromptu round of golf. Everyone was busy that day, so I decided to play a round by myself. It was the first time I had played a round by myself since practicing in junior high and I was excited about it. However, I also remember that as I played the round, it felt different. There wasn't anyone around to talk to about the great shot I just hit - or the bad ones. In fact, I caught myself saying "I hope I don't hit my hole–in-one today, because I won't be able to share the experience." Of course, I didn't hit the hole-in-one…it is still on my "Milemarkers ahead" list!

Research shows that if we want to have success in our workouts, our careers, and other areas in life, we need to have three things: A goal, an accountability partner and a "why." We all need three things, but the accountability partner can help with the other two. Don't have a goal? Let them know and they can talk through the process with you. Not sure about your why, same thing. It's hard to have success without these three things, but since the accountability partner can help you…start there! Double down in that area. Find someone that you can talk to and who will be honest with you and challenge you, grow with you, and *believe in you*. They can help you develop your ideas, execute your projects and move your career forward. As mentioned previously, sponsors are different than mentors - they give you more than advice. Sponsors help you move your career with opportunities and connections. Invest in these people every day to see the most return in your career and in life.

Who are Your Lifelines?

Director of Human Resources, Kim Pisciotta, was a guest on Episode 54. Kim is responsible for leading her company's HR Department. A few years prior to being on the show, I had asked her if I could bring my mentee who was in college by her office to visit with her about life in HR. During our visit, my friend shared some advice with my mentee that really stood out. When my mentee asked what advice Kim would give others, she said, "Know where your lifelines are." This advice is priceless. We always need to know who has been through similar experiences, or who knows who, or where we can find resources. It really doesn't matter what role you have in your organization or how experienced you are, we all need lifelines.

A few months later, Kim reached out to me and her text read, "I am reaching out to my lifeline." Her message absolutely made my day, knowing how much she valued my input for her question! I immediately responded. It's more than a career, when you can be a lifeline!

So, how do we develop lifelines? Well, we probably already have them, but may think of them as more of a personal resource or relationship. The key is to establish a strategy to develop more of these lifelines in our workplace. We need to get to know people in the office on a more personal level, then expand our network by attending meetings outside of our workplace. If we serve in HR, be part of a local SHRM chapter. Serving in mobility? There is a local chapter for WorldwideERC. Are you a sales leader? Become part of a networking group.

We can also find lifelines in our research with books and articles. In fact, one of my lifelines is a resource called *Mobility Magazine*, published by WorldwideERC. This is a great resource for mobility professionals and companies relocating candidates, and a great "lifeline" for anyone responsible for managing mobility. What about recruiting? Look for talent acquisition networks. Payroll? Yep, local payroll chapters exist too! There are resources for pretty much every vertical. We just need to have the courage to find them, take action and get started.

One of my favorite chapters in *Find Your Lane*, is called "The Carpool Lane." This chapter is about the importance of building our business networks. We are so much more confident in our roles when we know that someone we know and trust is only a phone call or text away from any challenge we're facing, benchmark we need to reach, or just to help provide some insight into our current situation. More importantly, the more resources we have, the more people we can help. Growing our resources creates a ripple effect. So where else can we find lifelines?

- Podcasts
- Books
- Volunteering
- Association memberships
- Conferences
- Church
- Social Media
- Family
- Business Partners
- Extracurricular Activities

Lifelines are everywhere. We are all filled with knowledge that we can share with others. We all have unique gifts. But here is the key - we need to share with purpose. When we share, we establish lifelines for others. We then receive lifelines in return.

So, who are your lifelines? Send them a text right now, or tag them in a post and let them know. Be intentional and make today the day you start developing your lifelines! Make a list of people that you trust and count on. Send them a note and let them know how much you appreciate their guidance.

Social media can play a big role in building community networks. During the 2020 pandemic, when many associations were closed down and not meeting on site, many people felt like it was much more difficult to connect and build community. Life was tough for everyone and networking was extremely difficult. But even though the environment changed, the process remained the same when it came to building community. We just had to be more intentional.

During the summer, I was asked to share a presentation for a virtual audience in Dallas, Texas. Following the event, a young lady named Rebekah reached out on social media to let me know how much she enjoyed my presentation. She then asked for a 15-minute call to talk about her current situation. She was changing careers from education to corporate human resources. She wanted my perspective on how to build connections in HR and have conversations with the right people to help her get in position for her next role. I shared how networking was all about connection, conversation, and most importantly - serving. It takes intentionality and a focus on serving others to build strong connections and it's a process that can often take a long time. However, if you are willing to go through the process, you can build a strong network of connections in just 30 days. Here is how...Reach out to connect with someone in that industry. Before leaving the conversation, ask for two referral introductions. You see, when you get a referral introduction, people are much more likely to respond to an email or take your call. This is a key starting point for anyone. When you speak to the next referrals, ask each of them for two referrals, and keep it going. Make sure you follow up and find ways to "be a giver" as a resource, providing value for them.

It really is true, the more we give, the more we get in our career. Approximately six months later, this young professional who began her journey with the courage to reach out and ask for a 15-minute call shared how she just landed her dream job in HR and was absolutely loving her new career. She met the right connection at the right time, but she still had to go through the process to get there. She later mentioned that being part of the CLIMB leadership community had also been a big part of the process for her, because of the connections and learning from others in community. Learning in community will build your network, and building your network will build your career!

Vice President of HR, Shannon Mosley (Episode 42) shared about the importance of networking as part of professional development. She has many different tribes that she can call upon when she has a need professionally or personally. They are her lifelines! Your network could be people in your church or people in your neighborhood. It doesn't matter, as long as you are purposefully building your network every day and building a community to learn from while helping others.

Lastly, Erica Rooney, Vice President of the Employee Experience (Episode 57) shared three things when asked about advice to share with others:

"First, never stop learning. Second, never underestimate the power of networking, and third, don't wait until the situation is perfect... because sometimes done is better than perfect!"

Thank You Batman

As I walked up to the hotel desk to check in for the evening, I was asked for my name and photo ID. I smiled and shared my name along with my driver license, which includes my full name - Bruce Wayne Waller. As the attendee handed me back my ID, he said two words that elevated the experience like no other. What were the two words? "Thanks Batman"! What was so extraordinary about this transaction was that the person behind the counter didn't just glance at the id and say thanks, but paused... made the connection with the superhero Batman and made me feel like I was important. I have had this happen a few other times, and every time I feel connected to that person because they paused for a moment to show they cared! Next time you connect with someone, pause... I mean really pause to find the connection and make the moment count.

Now, that is some great advice for building our community network.

What's Your Take?

Are you volunteering and engaged in your community? If so, what are you doing to grow your network? If not, now is a great time to ask others in your network where they recommend serving in community. Do you know who your lifelines are today? Now is a great time to write down the names of your lifelines and reach out to let them know. It will make their day and inspire more conversation in your community.

You're on the Air

It's Growth Day

Speak Your Influence

Build Your Brand

Building Community Networks

Turn It Up

Showing up with Gratitude

Recording with Purpose

Mic Up with Belief

Five Star Advice

Take the Challenge

CHAPTER 6

Turn It Up

"The best thing that energizes me is adding value."
Tonya Carruthers

If there is one thing we can turn up in our career, it's the volume of value. High performers add value first and serve like no other. I remember when VP of Human Resources, Connie Clark (Episode 56), shared how giving and receiving feedback - by looking forward - can add value for others. I have also had many guests on the show who have published books in order to add value for others, including Steve Browne (*HR On Purpose*), Dr. Derek Crews (*Mastering Human Resource Management*), Toby Rowland (*Unhitch the Wagon*), Mike Sarraille and George Randle (*The Talent War*), Tony Bridwell (*Saturday Morning Tea*), Jane Atkinson (*The Wealthy Speaker 2.0*) and Bob Stoops (*No Excuses*). There are so many ways to add value in the workplace, and serving others is always a great place to start.

Have you ever thought about the value of having connections in your career? As I continue my journey, I can't help but reflect each day on the value of so many connections! As a leader, connections are our career!

It starts as an introduction or acquaintance, which leads to a resource or business partner, and before you know it, you become lifelong friends. You see, connecting is more than a one-time relationship…it's an "all-the-time" relationship. So how do we take it from an acquaintance to a nurtured connection, or friendship? It starts with leaning in and serving, being curious…learning what's important to the other person and finding a way to help. That's adding value, that's serving. It takes time to build relationships and get to know people, but it takes even longer when we don't intentionally make it part of our everyday.

So how do we do this? We serve, and serve more, and keep serving. This is when the connection begins to deepen. It's when we become interested in them…really interested in who they are. It's about being intentional and purposeful, finding out what challenges them and what moves their sprit…then having the initiative to take action.

It's every day in different ways. It's a call or a text, a social post or a tag. It's a comment to let someone know you care. It's sharing things that move you as an invitation to come into your story. It's a note to say, "I'm thinking of you" or, "Hey, this might help you with that project." It's a text that says, "How are you?" or "You've got this!" It's an emoji smile or sports emoji that says, "We are on the same team today!"

> *Real connection is about serving, caring and being a lifetime resource.*

In John Maxwell's *21 Irrefutable Laws of Leadership,* he writes about "The Law of Connection." He says that leaders must touch the heart before they ask for a hand. Real connection is about serving, caring and being a lifetime resource.

Remember, as the popular saying goes, your network is your net worth. There is nothing that will give you a greater return in your career than investing in people. Make the investment and connect for life. So put down this book right now, make a list of connections and send them a text or a note, or call them. Use it as a bookmark for your book to remind you to make this part of your everyday! I am confident that investing in people will bring the biggest return in your career.

In fact, two of the most common questions I hear from organizational leaders are *How can I/we grow my network, my business, my career?* and *How can we get more customers, visibility, profits, etc.?* We should first start with the question "Why?" *Why is this important? How will this help us in our career?* If we don't know the answer to this question, the growth will quickly fade. The "why" provides our anchor.

When I was getting ready to write my first book, my friend Deborah Avrin advised me to make sure I had an anchor. It was my why. She said if you don't have a strong anchor, you may not finish the book. She said, "You will read and re-read your book so many times through the edit process and one day think – *is anyone actually going to read this?* That's when you will need the anchor."

For me, the anchor was that I was writing it to tell my story and to share my stories with my children and their children, and maybe one day with their children's children. I wasn't writing to have a New York Times best-seller, I was writing to create a book about my journey. It crossed my mind how nice it might be to give someone a book too. That was another anchor. By the way, the experience Deborah mentioned happened during the middle of the book editing process. I had that exact thought she had mentioned, and I remembered my anchor - which helped push me through.

Once we determine our anchor, we can then move to the importance of value. You see, to grow our organization, our networks, and our opportunities, we must start with adding value. When we add value for others, we find that we are valued even more. What brings people together, keeps them together.

I have had many conversations with people looking to build their networks. I always share the importance of finding ways to add more value by helping others as a resource. Unfortunately, many of us forget what value means. It's

Today we have more competition than ever, and if we want to grow our organizations, we must grow our people.

really simple if you look through the lens of the other person. The definition of value is "the importance, worth, or usefulness of something." Adding value can be as simple as bringing a smile to someone's day.

Today we have more competition than ever, and if we want to grow our organizations, we must grow our people. That starts with adding value! In Episode 55, Executive Human Resources Director Tonya Carruthers said, "The best thing that energizes me is adding value."

To do this, we need to stop pursuing and start attracting. We must learn to become more in our career, so we can have more to offer.

So where can we start? Here are a few examples of characteristics that create value:

- Friendly and Compassionate
- Creative and Connected
- Conversational and Collaborative
- Anticipating and Analyzing
- Inviting and Welcoming
- Resourceful and Relevant
- Service with Excellence
- Engaging and Encouraging
- Empathetic and Energetic

You see, when we give value, we will be valued. This inspires people to want to be part of our community, part of something of value! And the best way to start is by finding a way to connect, *really connect* with others at the deepest level. Many people will say people are born with this ability. I have found that this is really a skill. While there may be some truth to how people are brought up playing a part in their ability to connect, connecting is a skill. When we genuinely become interested in others and curious about what moves them, we can find ways to tap into that conversation. When I took my HR certification, it wasn't to practice HR, but to master this skill of connecting so I could be bring more value to others in the profession.

What about you? How can you start?

"Success is not pursued, but attracted." It's a saying I have heard and read over the course of my career that has been credited to speaker and personal development leader, Jim Rohn. How can we attract more success? It starts with becoming more, so we can add maximum value in every role!

How can you add more value this year? Start by giving.

Adding Value in Any Role

Author/podcaster Adam Grant shares a story about NBA Basketball player Shane Battier. Shane was a highly recruited basketball player in high school who made the decision to play his college career at Duke University. He won a national championship. When he moved on to play in the NBA, he noticed that he wasn't as talented as most of the other NBA players. He didn't dribble as well. He was much slower, and he knew he needed to find an edge to play in the league. He leaned on his knowledge and looked for different ways to add value for the team. One of his gifts was his knowledge of and ability to understand statistics. He could help the team understand where players were most likely to shoot from or how to guard against an opponent's weakness. It wasn't about his athleticism, but about **ADDING VALUE** to the team. (Work Life Podcast, Adam Grant)

The Giving Profession

When I joined Armstrong Relocation in 2004 as a new sales professional, I had zero business. I had operations experience, but no sales experience to get me started. So I read and listened to everything sales-related that I could get my hands on. Some of these authors and speakers included Zig Ziglar, Brian Tracy, John Maxwell, and Jeffrey Gitomer, just to name a few.

I also attended many conferences to hear these and other inspiring speakers along the way - Darren Hardy, Mel Robbins, John Addison, and so many others. I was thankful to these incredible coaches and teachers for showing me the way as I continued to build momentum in my new role. But I couldn't help but think...*wait a minute, if these men and women are such great sales people, then why are they writing books and speaking on stages everywhere? Why don't they just double-down, make more sales and build their enterprise? Maybe they aren't really as good at sales as they profess to be, so they decided to do something different.* I was so confused about why they were writing and speaking, but I kept reading, writing and grinding each day, and they continued to inspire me and fuel my growth.

I started writing in a personal journal in 1998, started a monthly newsletter in 2004, and then created a blog in 2011 that has turned into a weekly passion. I just kept writing. I also decided to enroll in Toastmasters early in my career to become a better communicator with both my team and our clients. I volunteered and got involved with different local organizations to expand my network and to become a better business leader. I kept showing up even when I was tired or didn't feel like showing up. I wanted to learn, grow, expand my network and hopefully continue the momentum in my new business role. I then began to turn my writings into books to share with others.

Fast forward to 2020...I finally figured out what they were doing...

> *It wasn't about the sales profession,*
> *– It was about the giving profession.*

The best of the best were just incredible givers. They learned how to connect with their audience, they found ways to give and give and give...and they kept giving every day! They wrote articles and shared them, they had ideas and shared them, and they created strategies and tips and shared them. They continued to look for ways to add value for their networks and for others in their path. I respect these men and women more now than ever. As I look back, I admire the way they connected with others that allowed them to give. I aspire to be like them as a speaker and business leader, adding value, encouragement, and inspiration for everyone in my path.

Are you in Sales, HR, Operations, Talent Acquisition, Finance, Accounting? Entry level to President - it doesn't matter - it's the same message for every role! We are all in the "giving" profession. When you show up each day, give your smile, your kindness, your ideas, your talents, and your overall best. Just keep giving! Your team needs you!

So, what's the takeaway? Keep showing up, keep looking for the connection, keep giving and getting better. If you believe in your message - share it with others! The best parts of life are the connections and the stories. People buy people, not ideas or programs. I love the journey now more than ever, and I hope one day people will say the same thing about me. "I saw him speak and he inspired me to take action. He gave and gave and gave and gave and for this I am better at giving." Keep showing up, keep giving, keep dreaming big, and keep loving your journey! I can't wait to see what's ahead for you!

How can you give this week? Use the 100/0 rule - give 100% and expect 0% in return. The results will be more than you expected. As George Halas once said, *"Nobody who ever gave his best regretted it."*

I Promise

A few times a year, Texas SHRM State Council members gather together from across the great state of Texas for our statewide meeting. Over 50 members typically attend, representing the 32 Texas SHRM chapters. As a board member, I always enjoy connecting with chapter leaders to review the business and chapter objectives, and to discuss ways to elevate the experience for members and guests in each SHRM community. We also talk about some of our goals, and the plans we need to follow to achieve our goals as the leader. When we finish reviewing, we then share a promise or personal commitment as the chapter leader that will help us achieve these goals. We call this our commitment statements. This is the ownership we take when we all agree on our actions to carry out the plan. This is another great way of connecting and adding value for others!

For example, I might say that I am committed to making myself available each month to discuss the current state of the chapter and to provide the support needed for success. Then the chapter leader might say, "I am committed to having 1-2 goals for each board member and reviewing them each quarter to stay on plan for the year." Commitment statements are great to share with your team in the workplace, too.

These statements remind me of a story from my book, *Find Your Lane.* Here is an excerpt:

Hold Yourself Accountable to the Plan

De La Salle High School, in Concord, California, was recently featured in the movie *When the Game Stands Tall.* This movie features head football coach Bob Ladouceur's teams, who won 151 consecutive high school football games from 1992 to 2004 - a record winning streak that stands today.

One of my favorite parts of the movie (and most impactful) is how the team prepared for the season during practice. Each player wrote down his commitment for the week on a small index card and shared it with another player. The other player would say that he accepted the commitment and they'd shake hands. Talk about POWERFUL!

What if we all shared a weekly commitment with our colleagues at work? It might be a commitment to getting reports in on time, returning all customer calls within a certain time period, or spending 30 minutes with a different employee each week to learn more about their stories and how to better support them.

When you prepare and hold each other accountable, you can accomplish things that you never thought possible. It may be preparing for a job interview or a sales presentation, or teaching a class. When you plan, you have a compass to guide you along the way.

What a great way to connect on a different level! Accountability partners are a great option. Do you have an accountability partner to talk to about strategy and achievement? Maybe it's time to ask someone you know to be your accountability partner. I absolutely love what HR Director Paige Lueckemeyer says in Episode 25, *"Never miss a chance to ask a question and learn something new."*

Inspiration, Desperation...or Maybe Just a PUSH

As I think about the workplace, I wonder how many of us had access to technology in this world of work long before the pandemic occurred in 2020, but just didn't embrace it for a variety of reasons. Many of us have had laptops for years and could work from pretty much anywhere in the world. However, when the workplace changed to working remotely, it forced us to learn this new way of work. You see, people typically make a change either when they are inspired or when they are desperate. Think about New Year's resolutions. We often make a list of things we are going to accomplish, then a month later when we see that it didn't last, we wonder why we did it.

We also change when we are "pushed" to try something new.

In our relocation business, we had "virtual survey" technology for a few years, but our belief was that we needed to travel to the home to survey onsite so that we could meet customers face to face. Our clients expected this and so did the family relocating. After several years of following this belief system, one of our company leaders challenged me to embrace the virtual survey model. I was doing about 100-150 surveys annually. That's a lot! Each survey takes approximately 45 minutes depending on volume, so with drive time it could take 2-4 hours to complete just one survey. To be transparent, I didn't really embrace this technology, because I was comfortable in my ways. The statistics showed that the virtual surveys were just as accurate as the onsite surveys. So, when the pandemic arrived in March of 2020, it "pushed" me out of my comfort zone to embrace the virtual survey model with our customers who were still relocating.

One week, one of my customers commented during the survey, "This is so much easier than I thought it was going to be." I was pleased that this technology could deliver a positive customer experience and we were still able to create a great connection. Since then, I have had many customers share how much easier and convenient it is for both the customer and surveyor to complete a move survey using this technology. In fact, the surveys are now recorded so we can go back and look at something in question during the move. I just needed a push.

It reminds me of a story about a wealthy man who was showing friends his estate. During the tour he showed them his swimming pool full of alligators. He commented that he had made his wealth from courageous decisions and if anyone on the tour had the courage to jump in the swimming pool and swim the length of the pool, he would give them anything they wanted. Everyone laughed and walked on until they heard a "splash." When they turned around, they watched a man swim the length of the pool and then get out. The wealthy man then said that he didn't think anyone would actually jump in the pool, but now that the man had, he would give the man anything he wanted. The man paused to catch his breath, and then said without missing a beat, "Good, the first thing I want is to know who pushed me into your pool of alligators!"

Now that's funny...and leads me to ask you - who has pushed you into doing something that worked out for you? Maybe it was to go on a date and you later married, to go on that job interview, to apply to take that certification or to join a book club that turned out to be a great network. Whatever it is, I want to challenge you to reach out and let them know how they helped you. It will mean so much to them, and even more to you.

I might have not embraced the new way of surveying homes if it weren't for that push. We also saw this in other areas of relocation - from virtual real estate consultations to temporary housing coordination to mortgage closings. It's everywhere!

I once attended one of our SHRM luncheons on Zoom web technology. It was super cool. The speaker did an excellent job sharing the content and connected with us by chatting with both the group and individuals in the meeting. This might not have happened if we hadn't been pushed into doing this for our members. After the meeting, we realized it wasn't nearly as hard as we thought it would be. I can't wait to see what this looks like in the years ahead. We are all just dipping our toes in the sand and we all know how quickly technology advances. We will probably attract more members, more employees, and more customers from areas we had never even considered.

So, what can we do to move out of our comfort zone and try something new?

1. Decide. We just need to make the decision that we are going to do it!
2. Make the commitment. Write down things you want/need to do.
3. Share with others. People will help you, but you need to let them know how. When we write things down, it increases our chances of success, but when we tell others, it is almost guaranteed success.

So many times, I have been pushed to move out of my comfort zone, and later felt gratitude toward everyone for helping me experience awesomeness. There have also been times I have been inspired to post a personal video, write a blog or book, speak in front of a group, or raise my hand in a meeting when I was the new guy. And, finally, there have been times of desperation - like looking for a new job. No matter the reason, you can do it. Make the decision! Be like Nike and "Just Do It." Your future self will thank you.

So, what are some of the ways high performers have shared about adding value on the *Life in the Leadership Lane* podcast?

- *Smile*
- *Serve*
- *Listen*
- *Do the right thing*
- *Be a mentor*
- *Recognize others*

- *Give feedback*
- *Coach Up*
- *Be transparent*
- *Share your voice*
- *Remember names*
- *Encourage others*

When the world trade center tragedy occurred in 2001, President George W. Bush made a speech to some of the people at Ground Zero in New York. The camera shows the President talking, then someone shouting from the back of the room, "We can't hear you!" President Bush replied, "But I can hear you." It was a big moment as President Bush showed not only that he was listening, but that he cared. As you can see, sometimes the smallest things can add the most value. Whatever value you decide to add this week, make sure to turn up the volume so everyone can hear you too!

Connect Through Serving

On August 8, 1982, a line drive foul ball hits a four-year-old boy in the head at Fenway. Jim Rice realized in a flash that it would take EMTs too long to arrive and cut through the crowd, so he sprang from the dugout and scooped up the boy. He laid the boy gently on the dugout floor, where the Red Sox medical team began to treat him. When the boy arrived at the hospital 30 minutes later, doctors said without a doubt that Jim's prompt actions saved the boy's life. Jim returned to the game in a blood-stained uniform - a real badge of courage. After visiting the boy in the hospital and realizing the family was of modest means, he stopped by the business office and requested that the bill be sent to him. This is what choosing to serve looks like!

What's Your Take?

It's time to turn up the value volume! How are you connecting on a deeper level? Where are you serving? What are you learning to teach others? If we want to add more value, we must learn to BE of more value. Find an area in which you can serve, connect, and grow. As you become more, you will find yourself sharing more and most importantly, connecting deeper as a leader!

You're on the Air

It's Growth Day

Speak Your Influence

Build Your Brand

Building Community Networks

Turn It Up

Showing up with Gratitude

Recording with Purpose

Mic Up with Belief

Five Star Advice

Take the Challenge

CHAPTER 7

Showing Up with Gratitude

"Always operate in a mindset of gratitude.
Our mind believes what we think, and our path to
success starts with our attitude."
Lynne Stewart

I am always grateful when I walk away from a conversation with a new idea or a different perspective that I learned from others. I guess that's why I like to ask guests about what they are grateful for before I end each show. When high performers and great leaders fail and learn to become better through it, there is a common thread - gratitude. That is how we learn. We learn through failure.

When I asked Executive Director Erin McKelvey (Episode 65) what she was grateful for, she shared how grateful she was for the difficult experiences she has had in life. She said life wasn't always easy and that's how we grow, by facing adversity and getting through it. She also included the mistakes she has made in business that made her a better person in the end. It reminds me of the words I once heard from NFL Hall of Fame player Chris Carter on *A Football Life*, "Every good man I've ever known has been through something."

The Best Investment I Ever Made

When I lean into gratitude, I often find myself reflecting on things that have shaped my life, one of which is reading books. Some of my favorites include: *How to Win Friends and Influence People*, *The 21 Irrefutable Laws of Leadership*, *Who Moved My Cheese*, *The Compound Effect*, *Tuesdays with Morrie*, *Little Red Book of Selling*, *John Wooden's Game Plan for Success*, and *Find Your Lane!*

Sometimes, I post a picture of a book on social media and ask others in my community networks for their perspective. One of the books I posted was *How to Win Friends and Influence People* by Dale Carnegie. While going through this process, I was reminded why this book was important enough to include in the top 7 books of my career.

In 2002, my company recommended that I take a Dale Carnegie Sales Training Program in Dallas, Texas. I had just been promoted to General Manager and I knew my time was going to be more limited. I also knew the course was very expensive, so I was grateful for the opportunity. I decided to take the class. It was scheduled EVERY Monday night from 6pm-9pm for 8 weeks, which was a major downside with a family. In other words, leave for work on Mondays at 7am and get back home around 10:30pm!

Many times, I considered going home after the long workday, but instead I drove across Dallas to the workshop in order to meet and learn with people I didn't even know. It was a lot of work, and as it turned out, it was more than a sales program. It was for leadership - an investment of time and a commitment to learn how to better connect with people in the workplace and in the community. The instructor taught strategies for "winning friends and influencing people" as a sales leader. I remember all of the times we practiced "people strategies" in breakout groups. We learned how to use people's names in a conversation. According to Dale Carnegie, ""*A person's name is, to that person, the sweetest, most important sound in any language.*"

> *The more we learn, the more we grow, and the more we grow, the more we can help others in our path!*

We learned the importance of being interested in what was important to the other person. People want to know we are interested in their story and that we care about them. The last week of the program, all of the attendees gave a presentation and I received the award for best presentation. I remember the time I put into preparing for the presentation and the joy I felt on my way home that night.

It turned out to be a short-term investment for a long-term gain! I knew early on that it would be a huge sacrifice of my time, but I didn't realize until I finished the program how big the gain would be for my people skills. Was it a lot of work? Yes. Did it take a commitment to finish the course? Yes. Was it worth it? Absolutely.

When I look back on that time in my career, it reminds me of what John Maxwell calls the "Law of Sacrifice." He says, "Sometimes we have to give up to go up" in our career journey! If there is an opportunity to invest in our career or "skill up," we need to go for it. The more we learn, the more we grow, and the more we grow, the more we can help others in our path! It also helped me gain a different perspective about my sales role. It's not about selling to people, it's about *serving* people!

My friend Steve Browne once said, "We are either spending time or investing time." What investments are you making in your career? It might take time to skill up your presentation skills as a speaker, get a certification, improve time management or planning skills, or just invest time to become a better leader in your industry.

You may not see it now, but one day you will look back and either say, "Why didn't I look for opportunities to get better?" or, "I am so glad that I decided to work on getting better." It has been the best investment I have ever made in my career and in my life.

It Wasn't in the Plan

Who knew the goals and plans we made in 2019 would be wiped out by March of 2020 due to the coronavirus pandemic? As I reflect on year-end planning in 2020, I didn't spend much time thinking about the plans that didn't happen. I didn't speak in three new states to help get me closer to completing a "bucket list" activity, and I didn't achieve my business sales plan. Instead, I spent more time thinking about how grateful I was for the things I accomplished that *weren't even on my list*:

- Increased stay-at-home mandates created more time to invest time with my wife and grandkids. Yes, some days were super challenging, but it also reminded me about what was most important in life… time is so short and I am grateful for these memories!

- Started a new podcast that connected me with so many high performers and amazing leaders. It was a gift to stay connected, visible, and educated in this virtual world of work.
- Completed a C25K program, and then competed in both a 10K and half marathon as I focused on health and wellness while our gym was closed. So thankful for the people who inspired me to start running.
- Learned and completed almost 200 virtual moving surveys across the US to help customers anywhere, anytime of the day, and to drive a better moving experience. Before the pandemic, I didn't invest time to learn the software. Little did I realize how much it would help our customers from everywhere in the world!
- Spoke at 27 events across the US about Leadership, HR, and Mobility. I had planned on speaking at less than half that many events, but the speaking tour doubled when we started speaking virtually, with less time now needed for planning and travel! I can't wait to see what the future holds as a speaker.
  ...and there's so much more to list!

I once read an article about a guy who wrote the shortest letter to the editor of the England newspaper, *Daily Mail*. The letter was from a guy named G.K. Chesterton and he was answering the question, "What's wrong with the world?" He sent the following response:

> Dear Sir,
> I am.
> Yours sincerely,
> GK Chesterton
> *(Story from the Maxwell Daily Ready)*

I love this story, because it is all about perspective. You see, a plan is simply "a guide" to get us to where we want to go... and to help us stay on track.

It's important that we spend time dreaming, setting goals, and planning, but it is just as important to acknowledge that we are going to get off track at some point.

It's up to us to have the right perspective to make a change, to adapt and try a different route. When we do, we find ourselves looking back and leaning into gratitude for the things on the journey that we didn't plan! We are the only ones who can choose to get back on track. Are you ready to get back on track? I am.

What can you plan this year that you will later be grateful for achieving?

Just "White it Out"

As a business professional, I attend a lot of networking events. I understand and value the importance of meeting people every day. I enjoy hearing people's stories as well as finding the connections during the conversation. Building a network is one of the most important things we do in our careers.

One of the traditions in networking is to exchange business cards. LinkedIn now has an innovative way to scan profiles for an easier connection on their platform, which is great since in this online environment, we cannot exchange business cards. However, people still like to exchange them when attending events in person. Some business cards are really creative, from the shape of the card to the messaging.

I once received a promotion in my company and needed to order new business cards. I was so excited about having the new ones with my senior manager title. On the day the cards were delivered, I quickly opened the box and pulled them out to put them in my cardholder on my desk. However, when I looked closer, I noticed there was an error with the spelling of the title. I was so bummed that I immediately called my contact at the company where I ordered the cards. When I told him about the error, without hesitation he replied, "Bruce, just white it out." I said, "Excuse me?" He said, "Yeah, just white it out – it's no big deal." What? I was so frustrated. I couldn't believe what I was hearing. Are you kidding? I went on and on about how it was not acceptable, and he finally stopped me during my rant to let me know he was only kidding and would get the cards replaced and sent over that week. I couldn't believe that I got so frustrated. Why was I so worked up over something so little? He was chuckling on the other end of the phone and then he said, "Bruce, are you okay?" He felt bad, as he was just teasing. But I thought *how did I let something so small upset me*? I had the expectation that everything would go perfectly, and when it didn't go as planned, I got frustrated. Isn't that just silly?

When I reflected on it, I realized that I was just having a bad day. I was a young manager trying to be perfect, trying to make my mark in the department, and I didn't realize how small this mistake really was. I was so embarrassed. It's such an easy fix. So, what did I learn from the call? Oh, powerful lessons that would go on to help shape my future.

First, I learned that I needed to be more patient. We all make mistakes. In life things don't always go the way we planned in our careers and our personal life. We need to be patient when we talk to people – both internal and external!

Second, I learned to have more compassion. We all make mistakes, and that's okay. My friend Dr. Sandra Reid always says, "Look for the 'bigs' in the 'littles.'" The big in this little was about having compassion. Listen to the story and find common ground. It's all about the story.

What stories are we sharing when we communicate with others? What stories are we sharing with our leadership approach?

In an interview with Success Magazine, Sara Blakely, CEO of Spanx, shared that when she came home from school as a child, her dad would ask her about failing. If she hadn't failed, he was disappointed. A lot of times we get down about failing, but this is where we grow.

I once had to reach out to a client to let her know that I had made a mistake on her moving estimate. I had forgotten to add something to the estimate. She didn't get frustrated. Instead, she was patient and allowed me to explain. She had compassion for me making the mistake too! I was very grateful for the understanding and made sure she had a great experience moving with us!

What am I saying? Be grateful for failure. Let's make patience and compassion part of our leadership approach when talking with others in the workplace as well as in our communities. ...and if it's a "little," let's just "white it out" and keep moving!

Grateful Leaders Inspire Action

In 2019, I went to a conference in which attendees were being shuttled to different venues on buses. As I got on the bus, the line stopped for a brief moment, so I asked the bus driver his name and let him know how much I appreciated him driving us tonight. Whether I attend a conference, facilitate a meeting, or speak with a group, I always try to be inclusive and connect with everyone in the room with a positive attitude and a warm smile. EVERYONE! First of all, we never know what others are going through and secondly, it's the first impression!

Early in my career, I had the opportunity to take a Dale Carnegie class to improve my communication skills. I was impacted by the importance of learning and using people's names when talking to them, so I make this a practice and use names as much as possible to show I care. I had asked the bus driver's name so that I could use it when talking with him as we traveled to and from the venue.

At the end of the evening, when I returned from the conference, I received a message from an attendee. She shared that a group of attendees had been watching and had talked about how I asked the bus driver his name and then said hello to him as I got on the bus. They were all impacted by that scene. I didn't know him, but I still wanted to share a warm greeting with him, too. I didn't know his story, but I wanted him to know if it wasn't for him, we would have been walking! I was grateful!

The message I received was meaningful to me, and it reminded me that people are watching us and the choices we make every day. We can all choose to be kind and positive, to connect, smile, and engage others. When we do this, others will follow. I know how special it is when people smile at me or ask my name and use it in a sentence, so I try to pass it on to others. In fact, when I hear guests use my name during an interview on the *Life in the Leadership Lane* podcast, it energizes me.

Today, I say THANKS to all of the people in my network who lead with excellence. You know who you are. You are authors, leaders in the workplace, colleagues, podcast hosts, family members, and friends. You are my clients, in my networks on LinkedIn, Twitter, Facebook, and

Instagram, and in my community. I see you and I am grateful for you today! I am a better leader because of you. Keep choosing to lead, keep choosing to be grateful, and make the choice to keep going!

Look for the Good

In the book *The Power of Moments*, Chip and Dan Heath talk about the importance of building peak moments. A peak moment is special. It's that point in time when you know something is about to happen. We feel the need to get out our phones to capture the moment. However, they go on to explain that it is easier said than done. The ideas are easy, but the execution is hard because nobody wants to take ownership. When we are willing to take ownership, we can create special moments to remember!

You see, when we look for the good, we will see the good. This is known as the Frequency Illusion, or the Baader–Meinhof phenomenon. It is a cognitive bias, a form of selection bias that says that after noticing something for the first time, there is a tendency to notice it more often. This leads us to believe that it is occurring at a higher frequency. It's like going to buy a new red car. As soon as we start driving it, we start seeing red cars everywhere. But it also applies in reverse. When we get caught up in the negative, it dominates our thinking and leads to negativity and even depression.

So, what are some things we can do to look for the good?

1. Find a way to help others through a donation.
2. Write a personal note and mail it to someone.
3. Find a puzzle to work on.
4. Invest in YOU by signing up for online learning.
5. Read a book and share with others.
6. Write in your journal. What are you grateful for each day?
7. Take a walk in the neighborhood.
8. FaceTime with family/friends.
9. Go for a run or workout.
10. Start writing your new book.

Take this time to reflect on what's important to you and make it happen!

Being Grateful for Values Energizes Us

We make choices every day. Some of the choices I made early in my career were failures, while others were not. Both helped me get to where I am today. But what drives our decision making? It can be influenced by the people around us, the season we are in, or short/long term goals. However, the common thread for all of our decisions comes down to our core values, our beliefs!

CEO Melanie Shaffer was my guest on Episode 30. When I asked her "what energizes you" in regard to her career, she shared that she gets energized by living her core values every day. What are her core values? She has narrowed them down to her top two – excellence and collaboration – and she is energized as she lives them out in her daily work. It was inspiring to hear her perspective.

It took me back to 1998. I was a young manager sitting in a training session when the trainer asked everyone to select our top five most important values. I was young and unsure about how to rate my values, but what got my attention was when the trainer asked everyone to raise their hand if "integrity" was number one on the list. I wasn't really sure about the value of integrity at the time, heck I wasn't sure what it even meant. But what I do know is that I watched ALL of the top leaders in the room raise their hand. That day, I knew the importance of core values and more importantly, the value of integrity. I also share this story to emphasize that *people are watching*!

Today, I include my core values in everything I do. I have many values - relationships, encouragement, achievement, inclusion, collaboration, compassion, and more…but my top 2 are integrity and continuous improvement. They are what energizes me. I have these values listed in my goal setting and business planning to remind me to think of them often. Years ago, I read the book *Dare To Lead* by Brene Brown and she shared that we should all narrow down our core values to our top two, so that when someone asks, we should be able to easily know and share these values. *Do you know your top two?*

One of my favorite times during my service as Chairman of the DallasHR Board of Trustees was being part of our core values design team. We went through a yearlong exercise to select the five most important values for our organization. It was time-consuming, and sometimes exhausting, but we wanted to do what it took to get it right. Now, I get to see it posted on the walls as you walk into the office. It reminds me of the importance of the time we invested in the process, and it makes me even more proud of the organization. This is energizing to me, because our values drive our decisions and make our choices easier.

Our company, Armstrong Relocation and Companies, also uses core values to drive decision making in all areas of our company. We call them our DNA elements. They start with Unity – We are better together. You see, they may not be called "core values," but you will recognize them because they are our beliefs, they drive decisions, and ultimately, they drive our culture! We establish values at our companies, but we need to establish them in our personal lives, too.

The key to leading with values is making sure both your personal core values and company core values are in alignment, which will drive your energy to new levels in the workplace every single day!

So, what are your values? Have you narrowed them down to two?

It's More Than a Piece of Wood

My friend Carl recently reached out on social media to let me know his dad had given him a piece of wood. It wasn't just any piece of wood. It was from the bowling center my parents operated as proprietors for almost 30 years, until it was destroyed in a fire. He shared that he hadn't done anything with it since his dad gave it to him, and he wanted to know if I would like to have it. Without hesitation, I said yes and he sent it to me. For some, it may not seem like that big of a deal, but for me, it was a piece of my history.

You see, starting at the age of 10, I grew up in the bowling center we called "Tri-City Lanes." My dad and mom purchased the 12-lane bowling center and moved our family across the state to begin their journey together as bowling proprietors in the small town of Seminole, Oklahoma. I enjoyed so many memories there, from learning to bowl, to my first job, to learning how to serve customers at the front desk, to cooking for customers in our snack bar (best hamburgers in town), to working on bowling lane machines as a mechanic. I bowled youth league with friends, sold school candy bars and gathered donations from the league bowlers who became our friends. So, here's the story.

Carl's dad's name was Bill Dodgen and he was one of the friendliest and most respected guys in the bowling center. He had a special way of always looking out for the league bowlers. He was kind and made everyone laugh.

But here's what was even more special. Each year, we were required to have our lanes "sanctioned" for leagues.

Sanctioning the lanes was a full-day process that happened once a year. When someone bowled a game during league play that qualified for an award - such as a perfect 300 game - the lanes had to meet sanctioning requirements by the national association *before the game was completed* in order for it to be an approved award for the league bowler. Bill and other members of the Seminole bowling association, including Harvey Cornelison, and R.L. Cross, helped handle this process. I also remember seeing Bill Houck, Charlie Padgett, Jerry Poff, Ed Hardin, Will Conner, and others there too.

They scheduled a date to meet early on a Saturday morning, and my dad opened the center to let them in. They showed up with levels and tape measures. They showed me how they measured the lanes, and how to tell when pins were good and when pins needed to be thrown out. My dad once shared a funny story about Bill and R.L. He said that if the lane was slightly off, Bill would say to R.L., "Just go stand on the other side…And now it's level!"…Lol!! That's the kind of people they were - genuine, authentic, and caring. They made it easy, they were true partners. They had also showed us where and when we needed to make important repairs. These repairs sometimes included cutting out part of the wood lane and replacing it with new wood...this is where this piece of the wood lane came from!

When I bowled my first perfect 300 game at the age of 19, Bill was one of the first to congratulate me. I can still see his smile. My heart is full of joy, love, and gratitude for these incredible memories. Maya Angelou once said, "I've learned that people will forget what you said, people will forget what you did, but people will never forget how you made them feel."

I will always remember how Bill made our family feel. I will always be grateful for these times, and for his son, my friend Carl, for reaching out to share a small piece of history for me to display in my office. And I can now share this story and others with my children and grandchildren! It's so much more than a piece of wood... it's my "lane of life!"

When I posted this story on social media, more than 100 people made comments about how this was part of their story too. So I thought, what if I would have not posted this? I would never have known how much it would have connected me with others or resonated with their stories. I connected with so many people - high school friends, teachers, business partners, customers, family and friends!

> *...when we share our stories, we open up a whole world of opportunities to connect and bring our stories together.*

Some people thanked me just for sharing the story, and some shared how this season of life made them feel. Others shared how they remembered bowling and playing pool and video games as they grew up in their hometown. I might not have ever known if I hadn't shared my story. You see, when we share our stories, we open up a whole world of opportunities to connect and bring our stories together.

So, what's a story you want to share that is waiting to be heard by others? Maybe it's time to share it with a friend, a colleague in the workplace, or on social media. Begin the journey of connecting with others. Spend some time reflecting this week on stories in your life. Write them down in your journal and share them with others when you feel the time is right.

10 things guests have said they are grateful for on the podcast:

1. Family
2. Health
3. Being present
4. Great job
5. Life
6. God
7. Relationships
8. Network
9. Failing
10. Mentors

So, what are you most grateful for? Write it down each day in your journal and share it with others. It will move you to inspire and change the workplace and your community.

What's in Your Blank?

A while back, during the Thanksgiving season, my grandson Crosby colored a picture of a turkey and I shared it with group of leaders in Dallas, Texas. The picture included a message around gratitude that said I am thankful for ("fill in blank"), so I decided to ask the attendees to fill in the blank. It's a great question for all of us to reflect on in our everyday leadership. So today, I ask you, "What's in your blank?" I am thankful for _____.

During this season, I often reflect on the time with our family as a child and teenager in Midwest City, Oklahoma...visiting Grandma and Grandpa Thornton. It was a joyful time, growing up with seven brothers and sisters and playing croquet and football with Uncle Roy. We ate Thanksgiving lunch at the kid's table. Grandpa Thornton walked around and visited briefly with everyone like a travel host, asking about our interests and making sure we were all doing well in school. There was a huge fish tank that grabbed our attention and we would watch the fish. Reflection is a gift. It takes me back to these days and gives me gratitude as I think about the stories I want my grandkids to share one day.

I am thankful for reflection time. As I wrote this book, I thought about how challenging life was for all those who came before me. All of the people, including my parents, who made the choice to sacrifice everything to provide opportunity for me and my family. I am thankful they taught us to respect others - who they are and what they value - and to always treat people with kindness because we never know what they have been through. *When we look for the good, we will always find the good in every situation.* Talent Acquisition leader, Christie Linebarger says it best in Episode 32, "I am most grateful for the people in my life; the people who have helped shape me and who have made my life better."

It's a great time to be grateful!

 What's Your Take?

What are you most grateful for? Start a daily practice of writing in a gratitude journal. Take the gratitude challenge at the end of this book and share it with others. You will be amazed at how it will take your days from good to great!

You're on the Air

It's Growth Day

Speak Your Influence

Build Your Brand

Building Community Networks

Turn It Up

Showing up with Gratitude

Recording with Purpose

Mic Up with Belief

Five Star Advice

Take the Challenge

CHAPTER 8

Recording with Purpose

"The work that I am doing today is going to make
life better for someone else."
Rose Ann Garza

Years ago, I was on a business retreat with a customer and several business partners. When the retreat was over, we all played a round of golf before leaving the area. During the round, one of the players, an HR leader, kept talking about all of the different places he had played golf around the US and abroad. I just couldn't believe someone with so many responsibilities had time to play so much golf! So I asked, "With your busy schedule, how do you find the time to play so much golf?"

He simply replied, "I schedule it."

That hit me like a ton of bricks. So simple, yet so powerful. Just schedule it. Since then, I changed up my planning each month to schedule the priorities first (which includes personal time), and then fill the rest of my schedule with everything else.

What about scheduling time to think, or write notes, or automate money deposits?

One year, I decided to create a time to be intentional about writing notes, book reviews, and LinkedIn recommendations. On Fridays, I look for the good in my network and post it. It can be a little challenging at times, because notes and recommendations take time to create. It's important to me to write something genuine and something that stands out, versus a canned comment. It seems simple, but it's not so simple, when we don't schedule it! We have to give ourselves grace when we can't think of something to write, or when we miss a day to post. We just have to try again at the next scheduled time. The key is to be consistent and make it part of every day or every week. The best way to do this is to automate it.

Create a system that makes it part of your work schedule. It's easy to do, and yet so hard to do at the same time!

I have talked about the importance of connecting in this book, but I want to make sure to share how it relates to automating, too. I want to talk about a deeper connection. There is nothing more rewarding or challenging than staying connected with people we don't see every day. I believe it's actually the best return on investment that you can make in your career and in your life. It's easy to connect, but it can be easy to get caught up in the day-to-day and forget about those connections, too. For example, when you attend a conference or event, you meet some of the most amazing people. Maybe you post some pictures and connect on social media. It's so much fun tagging and reading the comments from everyone, but then 6 months later, you realize you haven't talked to them since immediately after the event. Time goes by so fast, you continue to meet others, and the people you met at the previous event begin to fade away. This seems crazy…I mean you had an incredible connection with great intentions to keep that connection going. Why does this happen? It's because you didn't automate.

When we automate something, it becomes something we don't have to think about. Automating this is similar to getting our checks automated with direct deposit or auto-withdrawing for our insurance or retirement accounts. We don't have to think about going to the bank.

I am a simple guy. I have one calendar for everything - work, personal, etc. If you look at my calendar, you will see meetings, calls, vacation, networking, and connecting with people. Yes, you read it right… connecting. It might be time to write a recommendation, to reach out to a friend or family member, or to create a new connection.

But here is the deeper connection. Several years ago, I made the decision to make at least three people part of my every day. How do I do this? I send them a text. It might be a quote, or a picture or something that impacted me. You see, when it impacts us, it will probably impact someone we know.

Now here is the key…add people that you want to stay connected to into your phone, and when something reminds you of them, send it to them.

It's not about going down a list, but actually thinking about them each day. When we automate, it becomes part of our everyday. I send 3 texts everyday…not *some* days, *every* day! I once heard Zig Ziglar say, "You will get all you want in life if you help enough other people get what they want." It's true. The fulfillment from the return messages is off the charts.

Automating is executing a system to always live life in the leadership lane by staying connected – with deeper connections.

It's the joy that we are all seeking in our careers.

When we make the decision to automate things in our schedule, we become more intentional about things that matter in both our career and our personal life. In my book *Find Your Lane*, I called this "planning our roadmap." But this is more than planning. Automating is executing a system to always live life in the leadership lane by staying connected - with deeper connections.

So, what are you purposeful in scheduling?

Here are a few ideas for things to block out on your calendar, to help you automate your time every day:

- Reflection time
- Planning time
- Sharing appreciation with others
- Creating content to share
- Coffee meetings
- Making calls
- Posting testimonials or recommendations
- Personal/Professional development
- Writing book reviews
- Sending texts
- Vacation time

What can you schedule and automate this week to make an impact? Can you make it happen every day, or every week? What are you waiting on? Go ahead and put it in your calendar and automate it! Schedule something, and share what you're doing with someone you know, or share it on social media with #lifeintheleadershiplane! I would enjoy hearing from you! It really is true...what gets scheduled, gets done!

Time-Block It

One of the common threads that I have found when interviewing high performers is that they are intentional in using time-blocking to help them stay on track. CEO David Windley (Episode 7) talks about how we always have more things to do than we have time. He says that we need to know what things to say "no" to, in order to stay on track. Each day, week, month, we need to look at our calendar to make sure we have the *strategic* and not the *urgent* things blocked - or we will never get to those things. We have to force ourselves to block time, so that we will make time to get them done.

When talking to CEO, Melanie Shaffer, she shared about her "big three." She focuses on the three most important things she needs to finish that day, as well as her three "big rocks" or goals the company is trying to achieve each quarter. When she completes one, it is removed and a new rock is added. She adds these to her Outlook calendar to help her always stay focused on what's most important for her to win the day. In Episode 5, VP of Human Resources Seth McColley also talks about his three categories, or what he calls buckets. It is automated and helps him know what to say yes and no to each day.

As I time-block each day, I think about the question I once read in Michael Bungay Stanier's book, *The Coaching Habit*. "If you are saying 'Yes' to this, what are you saying 'No' to?" It's a great question to reflect on as you get ready to automate your day!

Automating our Well-Being

What about automating our well-being? Yep, we can do that too! Working on our self-care as leaders will help us be our best self. It needs to be automated so that we will make time for it. In Episode 39, CEO

Kim Zoller talked about automating her 21-day mindfulness journey and the importance of making this part of our everyday as a leader.

In Episode 44, HR Director Danny Bogard shared that well-being goes beyond health, and includes having a sense of purpose as well as managing stress and all that goes with it. In Episode 50, nutrition expert Allison Rezentes (Episode 50) shared the importance of health and wellness in the workplace. She talked about how creating a food journal can help us with tracking daily food intake, which helps us make better choices each day.

Being Purposeful

As I interviewed Coach Stoops, I had planned to ask him about purpose, but he beat me to it when he shared about his volunteer work with the OU Children's hospital. As he talked about making children feel important, he ended his comments with, "It's my purpose."

It can be really difficult to define, but it's so important that we understand our purpose in order to be effective.

I remember when I first heard someone talk about purpose, I racked my brain trying to determine what my purpose was. Early in my career, I went through many training exercises to write purpose statements. We have all done it, and most find it extremely difficult.

Early in her journey, my daughter knew that her purpose was to be a dietician and help others, I, on the other hand, didn't find my purpose until my late 30's. It can be really difficult to define, but it's so important that we understand our purpose in order to be effective.

This is another common thread between people who are living in the leadership lane. They know their purpose – their "why." I had an epiphany when I heard Camille Tate share in Episode 13 that she looks at our purpose as "being fluid." Every time something new or impactful happens in her life, she finds a rejuvenated purpose. I love this and agree whole-heartedly. We may have a different purpose during different seasons of life. We might have one purpose when we are single, and then when we get married and have children, we may find that our purpose changes.

I have come to believe that my purpose in my work is encouraging others to find their lane to create joy in their careers.

There are numerous resources – blogs, books, articles and business coaches, just to name a few - that can help you design your purpose statement. I'll share what I did to get to mine. I wrote down some of the things that were an important part of my every day, such as growing in my career, connecting with others in my network, moving people through relocation, but also moving people through encouragement to become their best. I get energized by so many things - hearing about a positive experience someone had, watching OU football games, bowling, being with family/friends, and helping people relocate.

I wrote down these words as part of my brand - Grow, connect, move, and energize. Then I put it in terms of what I wanted to do in my everyday: "Moving leaders to inspire and change the workplace." That's my purpose, my mission, and my every day. When I am in this zone, I am inspired and feel incredible joy in my life. I once heard that when you find the work you love, you'll never work another day in your life. I always thought that was a myth…but now I can tell you that it's true.

When your purpose is aligned with your career, you no longer feel like it's work! Isn't that fantastic? So, what's your purpose? Now is a great time to write down your thoughts and discover it!

A Daily Practice

When I interview leaders on the podcast, I like to ask them to share a daily practice that helps them to stay on track. I love this question, because everyone has a different practice that helps them drive everyday success. The common thread is they all have a daily practice, a "system" that they use every day, to stay on track.

Every morning they wake up, they don't need to even think about their next step. It's automated. It's not about copying others' practices, but finding inspiration in different things and then making it your own. A daily practice evolves over time. I remember being inspired to start getting up at 5am to start my day after reading a book suggesting it.

It takes a while to build a system that works for you. It takes trying new things, asking others for ideas, and building momentum over time. But one day, you will find your lane. It will become automated and your new system will help to keep you on track!

For me, it's getting up to exercise, read, write in my journal, and prepare for the day. It's about "winning the day." HR Leader Mandy Monk in Episode 37 talked about something she learned at one of her companies that has helped her. She called it a "detox." She literally dumps information from the day to decide what she is going to do the following day. Steve Browne is intentional about connecting with people on Twitter in the mornings. Angela Shaw writes in a gratitude Journal. Suzanne Myers reads the Wall Street Journal.

How do you "win the day?"

My Favorite Time to RESET

During the holiday season, I ask my guests on *Life in the Leadership Lane* about their favorite holiday. Is it Thanksgiving, or maybe Christmas? In Episode 34, Leslie Mensching shared her passion and excitement for Halloween, as her family decorates their yard every year with a theme. She gets super energized, watching the cars drive by their home.

I have always loved Thanksgiving, since we get together with family and share a spirit of gratitude. Christmas is one of my favorites too! When I interviewed Melissa Carrillo in Episode 33, she said her favorite holiday was New Year's Day, because it is a time when we all get a fresh start. A new beginning...a fresh start...what a gift!

As I reflect on New Year's Day, I think about how much energy I have during the month of December. I use this time for goal-setting and planning the new year. Most of us are involved in business planning during the year, but the personal planning zone is just as important. This is a great time to reflect on the past and dream about the future.

When I was a young manager, I heard John Maxwell talk about his goal-setting routine of getting out his pen and paper the day after Christmas. He used this time to plan because it was quiet in his home. All of the hustle and bustle was over. I loved this idea, and I have been doing this for many years as well. It's energizing to think about the things you accomplished over the past year, while dreaming about the future.

So many guests have shared the importance of goal-setting, including my friends LaToya Whatley (Episode 35) and Lauren Truelove (Episode 52). There have been others who have shared how they take this into the workplace and make it part of employee development. In Episode 57, Erica Rooney called this her PGPs. She has it automated for employees to opt in to participate in a personal growth plan exercise. This is so fantastic, because it puts others on the path to live life in the leadership lane.

For me, the end of the year is a time to plan - or what I call *RESET* - for a new season!

Reset is an acronym for **REFECT | EVALUATE | SET GOALS | ENERGIZE | TAKE ACTION**

REFLECTING and EVALUATING what worked and what didn't is a great way to get started. Then SET GOALS, building a "want to" list, and share with a few people to get their input for alignment and perspective. Take the list and identify the big rocks, the 2-3 most important things you want to accomplish by the end of the year.

This always ENERGIZES me and helps me stay focused on the big things. In business, we call these "critical success factors." In other words, if these things happen, we know it has been a successful year, and if they don't...well, then maybe it wasn't and we "RESET" once again!

Setting goals is our compass and helps guide our decision-making each day. It also reminds us of our purpose in life. After setting goals, be sure and include your values and personal mission statement. You see, this keeps "the main thing" - the most important thing - in front of us every time we look at our lists.

Now it's time to print the list and TAKE ACTION! This clarity of purpose, mission and goals is helpful during the year when times get tough and we might otherwise fall into "leadership fatigue" - taking our eyes off of our goals and our "why."

Planning ahead in this way also helps us to accelerate. Early in my career, I learned to plan annual goals and the activity needed for achievement. Later I learned to plan monthly, then weekly, and now daily. It's about deciding what's most important to you and setting goals to achieve those things in your career and personal life.

Here is what's amazing - we can all have a different way of scheduling things as long as we *do* them. I use my weekends for scheduling, reviewing my upcoming week and writing down important meetings, speaking events, etc. Then I fill in other times with weekly goals, including connecting with people, developing new content for speaking, and sharing information in other ways.

I include personal time for growth and family time in my schedule. Family time is important. It brings me joy to see others make this important, too. For example, I have a friend who makes attending opening day of the Texas State Fair a family priority every year. It's on her calendar and a special part of her every year.

When we have a plan in place, it gives us energy and makes it easier to "reset" when we get off track! The best news is that we can automate this too!

So, what's your favorite time of year? What do you need to plan? A personal vacation, lunch with a business partner or colleague, time to reach out with text messages?

When we plan ahead, we drive our life with purpose, decrease our stress levels, and create more joy in our careers. It's time to automate it!

Take 30 minutes out of your day and write down all of your scheduled activities for the upcoming week to get started. Then do it again next week. Set it up in your calendar so you can automate this practice.

Make sure you fill in some of the gaps with both personal time and people time to help you grow, connect, and move in your everyday. The people connection is always the best part. It puts you in the lane of fulfillment.

Over the Line

One podcast conversation that stood out to me was with CHRO Adrianne Court (Episode 27), when she shared the importance of "OTL" – which stands for "over the line." I absolutely love this. She said, "Many leaders will try to make it perfect - a project, an initiative, policy, event planning, etc. This approach results in them being stuck." Instead of trying to make it perfect, she suggests focusing on getting it 85% done and then making adjustments along the way. When we do this, we put it in motion and bring others into the story, while moving on to the next phase.

As you think about life in the leadership lane and the importance of automating things in your life, try to focus more on OTL instead of trying to make it perfect, and you will see things fall in line over time.

What are you ready to record with purpose? Start by writing down a goal and adding it to your calendar to make it part of your day. Automate it!

What's Your Take?

What is a leadership practice that you can automate in your everyday to keep you on track? How about your 401k or investments? How about your emergency fund? How about your quiet time, exercising or daily writing? Now is a great time to automate!

You're on the Air

It's Growth Day

Speak Your Influence

Build Your Brand

Building Community Networks

Turn It Up

Showing up with Gratitude

Recording with Purpose

Mic Up with Belief

Five Star Advice

Take the Challenge

CHAPTER 9

Mic Up with Belief

"Believe in yourself. You need to hear that.
I need to hear that - often."
Diane Sanford

Years ago, leadership expert John Maxwell shared a story about belief and perspective that has always been one of my favorites. The story is about a young boy who was practicing baseball. He said he was going to be the greatest hitter of all time. He threw the ball up and swung at the ball for a miss...strike one! He tossed it up again and swung...strike two. He then tried once more and swung...strike three. Then he picked up the ball and said to himself, "I am the greatest pitcher of all time."

Now, that's the perspective we all need to have when it comes to belief! Whatever we do, we need to have a belief that we can do anything we put our mind to, and I believe you can do that as long as you have the right perspective.

Of all the leadership traits that differentiate great leaders, I think belief is at the top. It's a confidence that we see with athletes in every sport. The gymnast, who has fallen off the balance beam many times, then achieves success in that pivotal moment. The golfers, who get so close that others count them out, but keep at it because they know how close they are before finally winning. How about the writer who shares the story about how they were turned down over and over until one day, their work was finally published and then turned into a best seller? Is persistence involved? Absolutely, but this persistence happens because of their unquestionable belief that they belong on the stage. You hear it in interviews when they are asked what it was that made the difference.

In one of my favorite conversations on the *Life in the Leadership Lane* podcast, I was talking with VP of HR, Jill Cole (Episode 45). She talked about some of the people who had believed in her even when she didn't believe in herself. This is so powerful. Many times, people that believe in us will challenge us to take actions we otherwise would have never taken, which ultimately helps us get better. Keep these people close to you!

Years ago, I heard speaker Zig Ziglar share a story about a cookware salesman who was down on his luck. The top producer saw potential in him and decided to try to help him get where he needed to go. All of the sales people went door to door to sell cookware. Some were more successful than others, and he wanted to find out why this person - with all of the potential in the world - was down on his luck. The conversation went something like this:

> "Do you own a set of the cookware?" asked the producer.
>
> The salesman replied, "Oh no, it's much too expensive for me!"
>
> "Oh, really?" the producer asked. "Well, how do you know the product will help others if you haven't tried it out for yourself?"
>
> "Do you mean you own a set?" the salesperson asked.
>
> The producer said, "Why yes…It was super expensive, but after I purchased a set, my sales started increasing because I could share the value they it was bringing our family."

The salesman decided to take out a loan and make the purchase. Eight months later, he was the number one salesman in the company. Now how could someone go from down on their luck to #1? Belief. Before he purchased the cookware, he couldn't share his belief. He didn't know it so he couldn't share it. We know when someone has belief in something or someone. It will move them to new heights.

A few years after I read the story, I helped a friend relocate. A salesman in our company made a comment that he would never move family or friends because he didn't want there to be any issues. I remembered the story Zig Ziglar had shared. This salesman in my company didn't believe, because he hadn't experienced the service. He hadn't connected with the moving crews and everyone involved. His sales never increased and he eventually left the organization. He didn't believe.

Believe in Your Dreams

In 1989, I was bowling for a chance to qualify for the PBA US Open.
The final game of qualifying, I rolled a perfect 300 game to make the top
5 finalists. Oh my gosh, I can remember the energy as I caught fire and
threw 12 strikes in a row…only to get eliminated during match play
finals. My dream of competing in the US Open appeared to be shattered,
until a last-minute spot opened up for me to compete with the best of the
best in bowling. It was excited, as I had been traveling across the US,
bowling in some of the biggest tournaments, to get ready for this event.
Now here I was, bowling on the lanes in the tournament that I had
dreamed about bowling in since I was a young boy.

As I looked at the standings after 24 games of qualifying, I remember the
feeling of disappointment, knowing I had finished in the back of the
pack. As I left the tournament, I thought about how my professional
bowling career was never going to happen. I am thankful for that. Who
knows how my career would have ended if I would have had success as a
professional bowler?

As I reflect, I think about how I just didn't believe. In local and state
tournaments, there were a few bowlers who were great. In the US Open,
everyone on the lanes was great. I struggled that week in so many ways,
but with my mindset and belief the most. I didn't feel like I belonged
with the best of the best. Maybe it was not my time, but I know now,
after many years of learning and experience, that belief often separates
the good from the great.

In business and in our personal life,
we often plan for something big to
happen, only to be disappointed
that it didn't happen. We may feel
like we aren't going to be
successful. In many cases, it's for
the best that it never happened. We
just don't realize it until later in
life. But belief will always be your
best chance for success. You have
to believe in *you*!

We have to believe and keep investing time to get better, so that we are in position when our time is called.

I remember calling on a potential customer for 10 years before they finally said yes. I believed. I remember being turned down to speak at events year after year before having someone say yes. I believed. We have to believe and keep investing time to get better, so that we are in position when our time is called. It will eventually arrive and it will bring more joy to you because you believed. If it had been easy, it wouldn't mean as much.

In what area do you need to mic up with belief?

Maybe you failed when you tried to pass a certification. Mic up with belief and try again! Maybe you weren't selected to speak at that big conference. Mic up with belief and try again! How about when you didn't get that promotion? Mic up with belief and try again! It's time to believe. If it didn't work out before, you just need to try again. In other cases, it's time to set some new goals and re-focus on what's most important to you.

Since competing in the US Open, I refocused my goals around family and pursued a new career in corporate relocation. It's been amazing. I have been able to develop deeper relationships with my family, my customers, my business partners, and my volunteer community. In fact, several people I initially connected with in business have now become some of my best friends.

So, when you get down because you haven't been able to accomplish something you have been pursuing, stay in pursuit of what's most important to you. Keep believing and planting good seeds. The good seeds will grow into something incredible in your career and your life. Life is an amazing journey when you mic up with belief.

The Power of "Yet"
I was recently listening to the audio book *No Pain, No Gaines* written by Chip Gaines, TV star on HGTV's Fixer Upper. He shared a concept that I believe is a common thread among high performers. He said that every time someone says we can't do something, we shouldn't stop there. We should add the word "yet" at the end of the sentence, to let them know there *is* a way if we all just think differently, think outside the box, and

work together in a collaborative way. For example, when someone says, "we can't do that," you end the sentence for them by saying "YET"! It's the belief that anything is possible when we get in the right mindset. Sometimes, we just have to think differently.

My friend Tracey Cade once shared a demonstration around this concept when speaking with the Lake Dallas High School football team. During his presentation, he talked about how easy it is to break a pencil - or even two pencils at the same time. However, when we bundle several pencils together, it is much harder to break. We can do so many great things when we believe, when we *really* believe. Sometimes it might seem like there is no way it can happen. This is when we need to step back, get creative, bring in others to help unbundle the situation, and break it down for success. Mic up with belief and it will happen!

Several years ago, I was hired to manage operations for a multimillion-dollar moving and storage organization in Dallas, Texas. This was an exciting time in my career, but immediately I recognized that I needed to quickly start building a team of leaders around me. I walked into a meeting during my first week at the new company and was told that we were going on probation due to poor quality being delivered to our customers. I thought *what a mess! What have I gotten myself into?* Our quality scores were in the tank and our moving claims were high, both of which were costing us large sums of money. In addition, our overall operational expenses were out of control. My first step was to hire an operations leader to assist me in training and developing our household goods moving crews. I knew I couldn't do it alone!

I had worked with a young man named Heitor Defaria at my previous company, and I knew he had the right skills to help me turn around the department. He was special and absolutely filled with passion. Thankfully, he was not only interested, but ready to immediately make a change.

Heitor and I began working on a plan to improve our quality scores and drive a better moving service and overall experience for our customers. After reviewing the current state, we decided on a plan that would begin with holding weekly training meetings for our moving crews. I asked

Heitor to set up the training room and prepare for the first session with twenty of our moving crew team members from the field.

When I went out to the training area to inspect the room before the session started, I noticed there was a small "broom" next to each chair along with a pencil, note pad, and tape measure. Heitor had taken the time to purchase one of each item for all 20 team members. I was very impressed and fascinated with the set up, but what really got my attention was the broom next to each chair.

I approached Heitor and asked, "Why do you have a broom sitting next to each chair?"

He looked me straight in the eye and said with passion,

"If we are going to train and develop our team members, we need to communicate and set expectations from the beginning. When they get in and out of the moving truck, it needs to be clean. When they move furniture in and out of the customer home, it needs to be clean. When they come into work each day, they need to have a clean uniform on, ready to start the day."

I was so impressed with his conviction and passion for building a team of excellence. At that moment, I was assured that we were going to improve our quality scores, as well as accomplish much bigger results, because I was working with a leader who was passionate about developing people to achieve business goals. Most of all, I was working with a leader who cared about people. He

Embrace the struggle. This could turn out to be your greatest moment.

believed! He believed in people, he believed in the process, and he believed in the organization....and I believed in Heitor. Our belief stimulated belief for our entire team!

I later heard Hall of Fame Coach Lou Holtz share that teams typically don't look for head coaches and leaders when they are doing good, they look for head coaches and leaders when they are doing bad and need leadership. Looking back, I now realize that life's greatest moments are not when we are at the top... it's when we are at bottom and we are building, shaping, and chiseling each day to climb to the top. Embrace the struggle. This could turn out to be your greatest moment.

What do you believe in? Better question, *who* do you believe in?

If you want to get the best results, find team members who have passion, the ones who believe what you believe, and make them part of the plan. If you are in HR, have a conversation with your business unit managers about who to include in the training and development. If you are in sales, talk with other leaders about strategies to include passionate team members to help you "clean it up" for success!

Disappointments and Setbacks

We have all experienced that moment where we thought for sure that we would be chosen for a promotion, speaking engagement, client partnership, or role on a leadership team, only to learn that we weren't selected. It can be disappointing and discouraging. When we have these types of setbacks, our mind races to different kinds of emotions which can lead to negative and even depressing thoughts. Or maybe you are part of a team, and the leader decides that they want to make a change and you are no longer needed. It can be pretty painful. What about failing a certification? Just as bad! It often diminishes our belief. This is when we need to get around people who believe in us.

I have experienced disappointments my whole life, from high school, to college, to pretty much every job I have ever had. I have been rejected as a speaker on multiple occasions. I've had clients leave our partnership. I have been excluded from a team leadership decision. I have failed an exam. I have missed out on a promotion. I applied to speak at conferences for several years before finally being accepted. Just because someone said no or rejected us doesn't necessarily mean they don't like us. It just means they are looking for something different from an experience or value perspective. We have different approaches we can choose, in order to handle this response for success in the future.

The first approach is to accept the decision with excellence and work on improvement. You can let people know you are disappointed, but also share your understanding and respect for the selection process and ask for ideas for improvement. Once you receive the feedback, start working on you. Jim Rohn once said, "If we want more, we need to become more." We need to use these disappointments as stepping stones for the next opportunity and mic up with belief!

The second approach is to turn our focus to gratitude. Great leaders are grateful. I once received some disappointing news that made me wonder if I was good enough or cut out for these moments. I reflected all day and wondered if I was in the right place, doing the right things, or even if I had the right goals. However, I kept believing and shifted my focus to gratitude – for my health, my family, and the people closest to me. I realized how much I had to be thankful for, and that I needed to just keep being me and looking for other opportunities to make an impact. I posted a note on social media that read, "I JUST NEED TO KEEP GETTING BETTER, THAT'S ALL!" Mic up with belief!

You see, when we mic up with belief, it is all about mindset. To have success, as we face disappointments along the way we continue to believe. We have to focus on the things we *can* control and stop worrying about the things that are out of our control. When we ask for a job or a promotion, the decision is out of our hands, but we can control our ability to learn and grow for the future. Whatever setback you experience, just remember that a set up for success is just around the corner. We just need to mic up with belief and keep moving forward.

Have you had a setback or disappointment lately? What did you do to overcome the situation? Are you still bummed about it, or have you been able to move on? Mic up!

Why Not Me?

In a country music documentary series by Ken Burns on PBS TV, he told several stories of famous people who moved the world through country music over the past 100 years. I noticed everyone shared a common thread. They all believed in themselves and felt a calling to pursue a life of purpose in music. Every single person had a belief and burning desire to pursue their dreams of being a singer or song writer. They didn't care about the challenges or sacrifices. They didn't care how much time it was going to take, how difficult it would be, or if they even made it to the top. They were just chasing a dream of doing something they loved - creating music.

I was moved by several different stories. Kris Kristofferson gave up a military career to chase his dreams. After moving to Nashville, he made many sacrifices, including working as a janitor, just to be in a recording studio. Willie Nelson produced songs for more than 10 years before anyone was even interested in signing him. Can you imagine how dark and lonely this time of his life was, wondering if he was going to make it? Vince Gill tried to make it for several years with no luck, and eventually gave up the opportunity to play lead guitar in the popular band Dire Straits to write and sing his own songs. Garth Brooks was turned down by every label in Nashville, only to be signed one night playing in a small café. He went on to sell 157 million records (as of 2019) - more records than anyone in country music history.

Can you imagine their confidence levels decreasing after every "no" and how difficult it must have been for them? But they all knew their *why*. It wasn't about being a star. It was about pursuing a career doing something they loved! They were all mic'd up with belief!

There were so many stories, and this is only one genre. So many other artists weren't even mentioned.

Another story featured Naomi and Wynona Judd. Naomi moved back to Kentucky after a divorce to raise her two children in a home she rented for $100 month. She gave her 12-year-old daughter, Wynona, a plastic string guitar to play while she tried to make ends meet as a nurse. They started harmonizing and singing together, at first just locally. Later, they pursued a recording deal. They finally got a record label to listen to them and to produce their first hit "Why Not Me" - a song which echoes their belief and which became their mantra.

Then I thought, "Why not me?" This is about belief to pursue a dream, a calling, a purpose. It's the stance we all need to have when pursuing our goals, our careers, and anything we want in our life. When we fail to make progress, or when someone shuts us down, tells us we aren't qualified or that we aren't good enough, we need to remember that it's just part of the process. Say "why not me?" and double-down on our efforts. It may take more work than we initially thought. We may need to put in more time after hours building on our craft. We may need to give up something good to go for something really great in our career. But if we want to be a great leader, we need to read about and listen to information about what it takes to be a great leader. If we want to be a speaker, we need to invest in growing our speaking ability. Whatever we want to do, we have to invest in doing what it takes to get there. Belief propels you to invest the time to grow toward your dreams.

- Do you want a promotion to Director, VP or even CEO? Why not you? Find out what others are doing to level up.
- Want to start a foundation to make the world a better place? Why not you? Now is the time to start investing your time and looking for people to help.
- What about landing the next big account as a salesperson? Why not you? It might take more calls, connections, or research to find the right problems to solve.
- What about achieving a life-long goal to write a book or to be a keynote speaker? Why not you? Start writing and start speaking at more events!

It's not going to be easy, but what great things in life have ever been accomplished without difficulties, failure, sacrifice, and hard work?

Remember these tips as you stay in pursuit of your dreams…

1. Determine what you want most…and go for it!
2. Know your why… it will get you through the tough times!
3. Invest time in your craft… It may take more time than you think!
4. Surround yourself with lifters… to keep you fueled for the journey!
5. Believe… and don't stop believing…in you!

And when you start feeling like the Hank Williams song, "I'm so lonely, I can cry," think about your WHY, your purpose, and call a friend. Imagine what it's going to feel like when you finally achieve it. It might get tough, it may be challenging at times, and it could even get lonely. But you will find that this is when the growth happens and the blessings occur. As Churchill reminds us, "The darkest hour is just before dawn." So, what are your goals and dreams for this decade? Write them down, and then say "WHY NOT ME?"

Believe in People

I once heard a story shared about Albert Einstein. The story goes something like this:

> *When Albert was a boy, his teacher sent a letter home with him to give to his mother. When she opened the letter, Albert asked what the letter said. She said, "Your son is a genius. Our school is not big enough for him."*
>
> *After his mother passed, Albert found the letter. It read, "Your son is mentally ill and he is expelled." Albert later wrote, "Son mentally ill whose mother turned him into a genius!"*

I am so grateful for all of the people who have believed in me over the years. My mom believed in me as a bowler. She cheered for me at every event. My dad believed in me so much that he asked me to be the president of the bowling association. My colleagues and clients, business partners, and so many others have believed in me. You see, when someone believes in us, we work harder for them and have more belief to share with others. This is the power of believing. It lights up someone's world when we tell them how much we believe in them.

During an ESPN basketball game, I watched as Golden State Warriors Coach Steve Kerr talked to his players during a timeout huddle. He said, "Can you see those guys? There is a lot of doubt over there, but over here it's all about belief." Then the camera showed the players and they were all lit up - ready to conquer the world.

Some of my favorite movies are about sports teams that had a leader who believed in the players and took them from good to great – all because of belief. I want you to know that I am aware of the work you are putting in by reading this book, and that I believe in you. Good things are just ahead. Keep going and keep believing in yourself and others as you travel though life in the leadership lane. The best thing you can do as a leader is share your belief.

Who believed in you? Who are some of the people you believe in? Go tell them and change their life!

Dream Bigger

I recently shared with a colleague a challenge that I was facing in developing a program for Texas HR leaders. We had a small budget and I was trying to create something for nothing. I leaned over and said, "Maybe the problem isn't our budget, but the lack of thinking big enough." He looked over at me, smiled and said, "I agree. We need to think bigger." Sometimes all it takes to conquer a challenge is a shift in mindset.

This has happened many times over during my career. When I shifted my mindset to think bigger and believe in the outcome, good things happened. So, begin to think bigger about your role and your career. In fact, when you set your goals, think really big by adding a "0." That's right, instead of growing 10% and working a *little* harder to achieve a goal, why not set your eyes on growing 100% and force yourself to find partners and resources to help you get there? This takes a lot of work, but more importantly - a belief that you can get there!

I wrote a poem one day as I thought about people who have so much potential but lack belief, yet are still in pursuit. My hope was to encourage them to keep going, and this is my wish for you too!

Find Your Lane by Bruce W. Waller

It's a long winding road on your journey to success,
but always remember that you can only give your very best!

There will be moments in time that mark your journey in special ways,
so embrace during the chase, or you just might miss the entire race!

You will find that the best parts will be in the people you meet,
the places you go, and the goals you achieve.

So, take the route where you can enjoy all of the sights along the way,
but if you ever start losing the joy, just stop to refuel
and keep driving toward becoming even more!

You may find yourself needing to take a detour on your pursuit,
but keep believing and driving with purpose,
and be grateful you're not having to travel by foot!

Is your GPS set to grow, plan and share?
If so, you will soon be there.

Be sure and pick up some friends that help you bring your best game,
because you will find the greatest moments will always be in the carpool
lane.

And when you have your GPS set and in alignment,
you will find yourself in the lane of fulfillment.

This is the best lane to travel and display a brand you can mold,
it says I'm genuine, I'm kind, I'm authentic, or maybe I'm really bold.

Yes, this is the best lane to be traveling on this race to success,
when you find this lane, you will find a journey that's better than the
rest!

 ## *What's Your Take?*

Who has believed in you in your career? Who do you believe in?
Have you shared it with them? Now is a great time to let them
know just how much impact they made in your life - at just the
right time and just the right place - to give you confidence to keep
going in your every day!

You're on the Air

It's Growth Day

Speak Your Influence

Build Your Brand

Building Community Networks

Turn It Up

Showing up with Gratitude

Recording with Purpose

Mic Up with Belief

Five Star Advice

Take the Challenge

CHAPTER 10

Five Star Advice

"The goal is not to be perfect, it is to be better."
Allison Rezentes

When I interviewed Chief Human Resources Officer, Angela Deputy (Episode 63), I asked her about the importance of challenging our team members to think big and speak up when they feel differently about a topic. She shared some of the best advice. She said, "In order to *challenge others*, we need to be open to *being challenged* as leaders." It was an impactful moment for me, and I have continued to apply her advice in my leadership journey.

Dustin Paschal (Episode 11) shared that when we aren't challenging team members, it can be viewed as "not caring." Asking for advice takes courage. It can change the course of the conversation, the direction of the organization, and sometimes even the path of our careers. This is why I ask all of my guests, "What is the best advice you have ever received, that you find yourself sharing with others?"

Years ago, I considered buying a used BMW, and drove it to work one day for a test drive. I walked into the office and asked my boss about his perspective, since he had been driving a BMW for many years. His advice was priceless. Contrary to what I expected, he told me that I might want to reconsider picking this vehicle. He shared all of the costs related to repairs and maintenance, and the limited number of shops that could work on the car. When he finished, I immediately drove the car back and picked out another vehicle. A few months later, my brother shared about how one of his employees who purchased a used BMW was always dealing with problems and costly repairs. He said the employee had so many regrets. I was so thankful that I asked for advice and took that car back!

I received some great advice in 2002, truly a game-changer for me as a young manager. I remember it like it was yesterday. One morning, sitting in my office as the new operations manager, I called my brother to tell him about the mess I had just taken on. I hadn't been able to identify anyone on my team with passion or even a little bit of positive energy who could help me turn around operations in the company. He asked if I knew anyone outside the organization who I could bring on board. I said, "There is a guy that I know who is not only positive, but he is also filled with passion." He was someone I knew I could trust with the task, if I could get him to come on board. My brother threatened me, saying that if I didn't pick up the phone and call him this afternoon to recruit him for my team, *he* was going to call him and hire him at his company. He said that in order to move a company forward, you have to start by surrounding yourself with great people you can trust and who exude passion, to model for others. He went on to explain that if you don't get the right people on board, you will be destined to fail and you will have a lot of stress and misery during the entire process.

That afternoon, I called my friend Heitor and the rest was history. Not only did we make our operations a success (as you read earlier in chapter 9), but we changed from a culture of mediocrity to a culture of excellence. Heitor helped transform our operations by hiring the right people, setting expectations, and holding each person accountable along the way. His positive energy was infectious and he made his team feel like they were valued and part of something special - like family.

A few years later, when I decided to make a career change and move to a new company, my brother hired Heitor and he transformed his company operations too. *It's always about people, and it will always be about people!* People who have passion, people you can trust, people who care, people who believe, and people who want to make a difference.

Jimmy Valvano shared in his infamous speech all of the things we need to do every day. During the speech at the ESPYS, he stated that we all need to laugh, we all need to think, and we all need to be moved to tears every day. "If you laugh, you think and you cry, that's a full day...You do that seven days a week, you're going to have something special."

People who share advice are special. They help us to see through a different lens, and by being more open to advice, we become better resources for others.

As I reflect on all of the advice I have received on *Life in the Leadership Lane* podcast and throughout my career, I am filled with gratitude. I am a better leader because of the advice I have received and applied. What is interesting is that we can find advice everywhere - we just have to be open to listening, receiving, and applying what works for us. The more we listen, the more we will hear. The more we hear, the more we can apply. The more we apply, the more we can share with others. This is how leaders make an impact on *Life in the Leadership Lane*!

> *Advice can help us grow, teach us life lessons, and help us fail, so that we can use that experience to get better.*

There are so many moments that I look back on and say, *that is when I heard this* or *that is when I tried this*, and the event has made an impact on my career. This is the reason I make this question part of my every day. We can learn so much from others. Advice can help us grow, teach us life lessons, and help us to fail, so that we can use that experience to get better. What's even more remarkable is that when you ask people about critical advice they have received, they remember the moment, the person, the book, or the situation. That is why sharing it is so important. When we share, we impact others! We don't have to wait until someone asks us, we can create opportunities and use stories to share every day!

One Brick at a Time

When I was in high school, we had a really good defense. It was one of the best defenses in the state of Oklahoma. At one point, we posted seven straight shutouts. Our fans started referring to our defensive team as "the green brick wall." When you attended football games on Friday nights at Seminole Chieftains stadium, you saw banners lined up on the chain link fence with pictures of bricks. There were also signs all over downtown, fueling the football community. It was both energizing and inspiring.

As I think about the advice that has been shared by guests on *Life in the Leadership Lane* and by others in my career, I think about how great leadership starts with just one brick. It's a brick of advice that provides us a starting point to build our career. Then we find another brick to add, then another, and another, and one day we look and realize we have a wall of bricks of advice that has made us who we are. Think about all of the great advice you have received over your career, and not-so-great advice that was used as teaching moments. Advice is how we gain our toughness and resilience in the hard times, and stay grounded through the successes. So, draw a rectangular shape of a brick and write down the best advice you have ever received, then draw another, and write down another favorite. Create a brick wall with some of the advice you have received during your career and post it on your wall. One day you can look back and remember how it all started with that first brick!

Now, let's take a look at *Life in the Leadership Lane's* **"Brick Wall of Leadership"**

| *You can't be successful without failures.* Chrissie Rogers | *You have to lead by example. You can't ask from others things you don't require of yourself.* LaTonya McElroy | *Trust is the currency to any human relationship.* Jimmy Taylor | *True change comes from individual behavior.* Angela Shaw | *Leaders make other people feel valued.* Steve Browne | *When you seek out relationships, and stay in a growth mindset, you can find mentors anywhere.* Annie Carolla | *It's okay to fail, because that is how we learn.* Lianne Daues | *Believe in people, even when they don't believe in themselves.* Jill Cole | *Well-being is doing the things you love doing, while managing all of the things you need to get done.* Danny Bogard | *I did think I knew a lot about disability and inclusion space until I started participating.* Mary Leone | *This year more than ever, we need to be armed with a pencil and a big eraser.* Melissa Goebel | *Partnering and being a subject matter expert is the core of being a good recruiter.* Shannon Mosley | *When you work hard and deliver, things start happening for you.*

Suzanne Myers | *Inclusion is about bringing yourself to the table in fullness.* Halima K. McWilliams | *It's critically important that people know who we are, and what we are about, and we know who we are, and what we are about.* Kim Zoller | *Every experience you have is a lesson learned.* Mandy Monk | *It's not the product, it's the finished product.* Martha E. Thornton | *There is a lot of power in saying yes.* Seth McColley | *Just because you don't have a certain title doesn't mean you're not a leader.* LaToya Whatley | *Everyone needs to know they deserve to be in the room and have a voice.* Tyra Bremer | *A high performing team is people that challenge one another.* Dustin Paschal | *Use your values to shape decisions.* Greg Hawks | *If you're feeling like there is something you want to chase, a dream, something to do – go do it.* Paige Lueckemeyer | *The most satisfying thing about leadership is you get to help others achieve their goals.* Melissa Carrillo | *We are all looking to give back and that's what volunteering is.* Kathy Hardcastle | *Baby steps are sometimes the best when you set out to accomplish a goal.* Lynne Stewart | *When you start looking at the big picture and you start looking at the impact your job makes, it is transformational.* Christie Linebarger | *Try to reach for that brass ring, even if it's a little out of reach.* Janet Hanofee | *Be a student, be a solution, and be sustainable.* Mitch Beckman | *Simply say, thank you.* Jamie Son | *The work that I am doing today is going to make life better for someone else.* Rose Ann Garza | *Don't let rejection tell you that you're not great.* Camille Tate | *The work that I am doing helps me live my two core values every single day.* Melanie Shaffer | *High performing teams are ones that treat employees like customers.* Yvonne K. Freeman | *Teams that work really well together get charged up because they believe in the goal they are going after, and they believe in how they are going to get there.* Diane Sanford | *We are where work is going.* Lynn Shotwell | *Always approach your job with the lens of a CEO.* David Windley | *Empower everyone and let them feel invested.* Toby Rowland | *Developing people will develop your culture.* Kevin Dawson | *Bring the fun and work can be fun.* Jessica Heer | *Be yourself.* Ed Curtis | *Do the right thing.* Ray Kallas | *Don't judge a book by its cover.* Mike Sarraille | *Be a talent magnet.* George Randle | *Enjoy the moment.* Denise Snow | *Job readiness is about being ready all the time.* Kelvin Goss | *Focus on the steps, not the fall.* Tony Bridwell | *The goal is not to be perfect, it's to be better.* Allison Rezentes | *When the door closes, find a window to break.* Adrianne Court | *It's a mindset shift to move away from I am right and this is how things should be done, to having open mindedness.* Erica Rooney | *A leader is somebody who's really going to bring people along and lift others up.* Connie Clark | *Leadership is achieving results with and through others.* Tonya Carruthers | *If you want something, ask for it.* Kim Pisciotta | *Anybody - no matter what their position - can be a leader formally or informally.* Lisa Collins | *It's important to give back what we've been given.* Lauren Truelove | *The NO is leading me to the right YES.* Leann Day | *See people where they are and meet people where they are.* Leslie Mensching | *Leadership is an honor and a privilege.* Nicole Roberts | *Find happiness in the intersection between helping people grow, connectivity and creativity.* Shawn Storer | *We can't serve without connecting, and we can't connect without serving.* Bruce Waller | *Every position is a learning opportunity.* Jennifer Swisher | *Learning has not occurred until behavior has changed.* Dr. Derek Crews | *Everyone wants a voice.* Kim Kneidel | *Leadership is to be in service for others.* Angela Deputy | *If I can make this person's day just a fraction easier, they are going to remember that long term.* Justin Dorsey | *Don't be afraid to ask for help.* Erin McKelvey | *If you are growing with the company, you are growing the company.* Dustin Jones | *My purpose is to be of service to others.* Nicole DiRocco | *Tell a story. You need to showcase how you are a difference maker.* Jimmy Richards |

Care about people first. Holly Novak | *Follow your Passion.* Brian Yanus | *Choose your inner circle wisely.* Bronwyn Allen | *Don't be afraid to change it up for improvement.* Bob Stoops | *Be true to yourself.* Jed Gifford | *Always be looking for the next step.* Adam Waller | *Look for the gold in other human beings.* Carol Kiburz | *If you're not ready to fail, you're not ready to scale.* Jane Atkinson | *Words really do matter.* Rachel Kennedy |

Now That is "5 Star" Advice

The advice and lessons shared on the *Life in the Leadership Lane* podcast remind me of a quote shared by Dallas Baptist University student Kragen Kechely during a leadership presentation. He said, "Success leaves crumbs." What crumbs of success can we pick up from high performers that live life in the leadership lane? Here are some crumbs to consider on your personal journey:

Believe in yourself.

Collaboration is better.

Values make decisions easier.

It's not how we start, but how we finish.

Empowering your team will create engagement.

Intentional leaders use a system.

Use "fun" to engage your group.

Mentors are great, but sponsorship can be better.

Your voice matters.

Be a good listener.

Be yourself.

Set goals and try to get better every day.

Don't be afraid to fail.

It takes hard work to have success.

Enjoy the moments.

Say Thank you.

Make networking part of your everyday.

Getting better takes practice.

What will we learn over the next 100 (or add that "0" and make it 1,000) episodes, or through our everyday conversations with others? When we are intentional, we will always find learning opportunities to help us live every day of life in the leadership lane. I can't wait to learn more and share with others along the way.

What Will Your 10-years-older Self Ask You?

At the end of every show, the last question I like to ask my guests is, "What would your 10-years-older self ask you if he or she were knocking on your door right now?" The answers are always uplifting and sometimes emotional, as guests think about how they have been living their life in the leadership lane...if their 10-years-older self would be proud, or would just want them to know it's going to be okay. A few guests have laughed and others have even shed some tears. It's such a great reflective question.

> *...it's not about the things we want to achieve, it's about the person we want to be.*

Are we doing the little things in life that our future self will be proud of, or do we need to change lanes and get back on track? I always try to emphasize in those moments, that it's not about the things we want to achieve, it's about the person we want to be.

Years ago, when I started setting goals, I wanted to achieve so many things in my career. I still do. I've won many awards for my work. I've won many awards for bowling. However, I think my 10-years-older self would tell me that he is proud of the person I have become in the workplace and most importantly, in my personal life. He would also say, "Keep going, keep growing, keep connecting, and keep serving others. You have important work ahead."

In 2014, I was presented with the prestigious *Saul Gresky Award*, which is an award presented to the North Texas Relocation Professional of the Year. It is presented to one individual each year who best exemplifies the tradition of high customer satisfaction and service to relocation of corporate employees, makes a major contribution to the positive image of the relocation profession, and inspires cooperation and support among members of the relocation industry. It's not about titles or numbers, it's about contribution and service. I remember thinking as I received the award...*This is what I was going for early in my career when I was trying to find my lane and purpose.* I have always just wanted to add value to others and be respected in my industry by doing things the right way. Working hard, being resourceful, and treating people with kindness. I was only there because of the people who had shown me the way, role-modeled what good leadership looks like and inspired me to become my best self.

Who inspires you? Who do you want to be more like? This is a great starting point for anyone in any role in their career. Always start with people. Surround yourself with those who inspire who you want to be!

In the spring of 2021, I was recognized by Benivo for being in *The Global Mobility Top 100 Most Admired Service Providers of 2021.* It was truly an honor, and I know my 10-years-older self would still say, "Well done, keep going, keep connecting and keep serving!" There were over 4,000 nominations from around the world! I felt very proud to be included in this amazing group of talented professionals in my industry. I remember when I learned I had received the award. I was sitting at my desk, and I received a text from my friend Pam in Chicago that said, "Congrats on being one of the elite!" I checked out Benivo's top 100 list and saw my name. I was proud to be included with so many industry giants. Many were role models for me in my career. **It's not about being the best, it's about living our best, doing our best, and giving our best.** This is what *Life in the Leadership Lane* is all about. It's moving people to inspire and change the workplace. Honor and learn from the people who inspire you.

A New Year, a New Hope

As I conclude, I want to share a story... When my book *Find Your Lane* was published back in 2017, I was asked to speak for a real estate association in Fort Worth, Texas. The group wanted me to kick off the year with a motivational message for their members attending. I was excited to be asked and agreed to speak. On the day of the event, I shared with the group my thoughts on the topics of goal setting, networking, and driving a career with purpose. It was a good meeting with about 75-100 attendees. There were a few laughs and people seemed to be engaged during the meeting.

When the meeting finished, several people came up and shared how much they enjoyed the presentation. I was glad to be able to add some value for them. However, one lady's comment stood out and reminded me of my why. She said, "Thank you for your presentation. I want you to know that today, you gave me hope." I was full of joy but wanted to know more, so I asked her to share more about how the message gave her hope. She went on to share that her husband had been diagnosed with stage 4 colon cancer, which had left her without hope. She put her dreams and plans on the back burner and thought they would be there forever. She now had the courage to move forward despite the outcome. She later posted a review so that I would always remember how I made her feel that day… here is the post:

5.0 out of 5 stars

Reviewed in the United States on January 26, 2018 on Amazon

This book gave me hope. My husband facing stage 4 colon cancer left me without a lane. Dreams and plans on the back burner. Bruce's book gave me the courage to pick a lane and move forward in 2018 despite the outcome...Thank you for this book!

It was one of the most inspiring moments of my career and reminded me that we never know what people are going through. We never know who might be watching or listening. We never know when it's going to be the right time or right moment for someone to receive our message from our story. It might not seem like we are ever getting through or making impact. But one day, you may find yourself sharing hope as a leader.

My hope is that this book has inspired you to choose to lead when you are on the air, make every day a growth day, develop your influence, build a brand that matters to you, develop yourself so you can develop others, turn up the value, be grateful for every day, record your day with purpose, and believe in yourself and others. Traveling through life in the leadership lane is energizing and so amazing. Now it's time to accelerate, because our most important work is just ahead of us!

What's Your Take?

What is some advice you have been given that was so good you find yourself wanting to share it with others? Write it down and share it with your colleagues, family, and friends! Start your own leadership brick wall of advice! Let the person who shared it with you know how it has impacted your life.

You're on the Air

It's Growth Day

Speak Your Influence

Build Your Brand

Building Community Networks

Turn It Up

Showing up with Gratitude

Recording with Purpose

Mic Up with Belief

Five Star Advice

Take the Challenge

Take the Challenge

"It's not just my willingness to challenge,
it's my willingness to be challenged.
That starts with me as a leader."
Angela Deputy

I once heard that knowledge is useless without execution. When we put something we learn into action, we start building momentum and creating energy to help us move forward in both our personal life and our career. When we challenge ourselves, we stretch ourselves, we feel energized, we build confidence, and we engage with others during the process. I have embraced many challenges in my career. I can remember each one of them because of the stories we shared during the experience. Just a few of the many challenges I have accepted include exercise challenges, writing challenges, and food challenges. Each one has shaped me and helped me to become more in every area of my life.

One year, my son-in-law Chase asked me to do the "Murph challenge" with him and my sons. I said yes! It's one of many workout challenges that are held across the US on Memorial Day to honor our fallen soldiers. The Murph Challenge is more than just a workout. It's a tradition that helps people dedicate a bit of pain and sweat to honor LT Michael P. Murphy (SEAL), a man who sacrificed everything he had for our freedom. It includes running, pushups, pull ups, and squats. It was raining that day and I remember how hard it was to complete the workout. But we now have a deeper connection from sharing that moment, another story that binds us together because of the challenge. The following year, we completed another challenge called the *"MAUPIN"* workout, to honor another soldier. We plan to continue these and other challenges each year.

When we talk about a challenge, it takes us back to that moment. Challenges create growth, increase engagement, and build experience in life. Now that you are ready to live life in the leadership lane, I want to challenge you to become more by accepting or creating a challenge for you and for people on your team or in your community network. I am confident that when you commit, *really* commit to a challenge, you will grow, you will engage, and you will move other leaders to inspire and change the world around them!

On the following pages, I have shared a variety of Challenges. Choose a challenge that resonates with you and begin your journey to become more!

Are you ready?

Let's go!

1-DAY CHALLENGE
A challenge you can accomplish in one day.
Suggestions:

> *Walk/Run 1 mile, 5k, 10k or half marathon.*
> *Spend the day setting some goals.*
> *Spend the day building a vision board.*
> *Write a blog about your industry.*
> *Take a day off with your team to build relationships.*

30-DAY CHALLENGE
A challenge you can work on each day, consistently, for a month.
Suggestions:

> *Get up earlier to practice a discipline.*
> *Send a thank you note every day.*
> *Write a recommendation to people in your network.*
> *Keep a food journal.*

Create one idea a day that will help your company.

Make a call every day to a family/friend.

Text something inspirational to three people every day.

1-YEAR CHALLENGE
A challenge you can work on over the course of the next year.
Suggestions:

Read a book every month.

Write in a journal every day.

Practice a musical instrument.

Take a picture a day to build a year of moments.

I would enjoy building on these lists. If you have an idea, tag me in a social media post with #LifeInTheLeadershipLaneChallenge

CREATE YOUR NAME CHALLENGE
Write down your name in a vertical format and identify a word for each letter - customized for you! Here is an example I shared with my dear friend Dr. Sandra Reid, Chair of Graduate School of Business at Dallas Baptist University:

S Strategic

A Anticipates

N Never Stops Learning

D Determined (and DBU)

R Relational

A Amazing

Once you complete it, share it with others to engage in conversation, use it as a team building exercise, or post on your wall as a daily reminder. Thanks for the challenge Steve Browne!

FIND YOUR BRAND CHALLENGE

Ask people in your network to share three words that come to mind when they think of you. Do this on social media or in the workplace. Once completed, copy all of the words, place into a word art program and watch which words populate into your brand! Then share with others. I also shared this with my sister-in-law, Lesa Ivey, and she used the exercise to engage her team at work. Each person wrote down the words on a piece of paper and she created word brands for everyone on her team. It's a great way to create engagement and drive conversation with others, while helping you identify and live your brand! Thanks for the challenge, Jennifer McClure!

QUESTION LOG CHALLENGE

As I mentioned in chapter 3, a great way to develop influence and build relationships is to keep track of questions. When you get the same questions over and over, turn it into an opportunity to share with your leadership team. It may be time to update a policy or start something new to make your workplace better for everyone. It also shows others you are listening.

LETTER CHALLENGE

Personal letters are one of the most powerful ways to impact people. Many years ago, it was common to send and receive letters in the mail. At that time, we didn't have computers to share notes and letters electronically with our family and friends. Today, we often use social media outlets because it is easy and saves us time, but there is something special and even magical about receiving a personal letter from a family member or friend.

In *Find Your Lane*, I talked about the importance of writing personal letters. I have been sending personal notes and letters for many years. I have received many too, including a letter I received from the 43rd President of the United States, George W. Bush. It is meaningful when we receive a letter, because we know and understand the time and effort it takes to write and mail a note. People who mail letters often never know how much their kind note impacted others.

Letters create deeper connections between people. Because of this, many of us keep letters we receive from family and friends for life. A few years ago, I read an inspiring letter in the paper. It was an open letter from a daughter to her father, Payne Stewart, who was tragically killed in a plane crash at the age of 42. Payne Stewart was a professional golfer who played in college at Southern Methodist University in Dallas, Texas, and later became one of the best professional golfers on the PGA tour. He was one of my favorites. When I read her letter on social media, I felt inclined to respond with this comment on my social media page.

> *"When I read this letter, it not only filled my eyes with tears, but also provided reflection on some of the things I am most grateful for: The day I walked my daughter down the aisle, the day my oldest son told me he had found his true love, and the day my youngest son showed how he was no longer embarrassed to have his dad around by putting his arm around me during warm-ups on the football field in his senior year. This tribute reminds me of all the wonderful things we get to experience in life that we sometimes take for granted. My hope is that we can all model great character for our children like Payne Stewart did during his time here...so inspiring! My eyes are full of tears now and my heart is full of love for my family - and for his family. He was one of my favorites, and reading this letter makes him even bigger than life today."*

The letter is titled "Miss You Everyday" and you can read it here: https://www.pgatour.com/long-form/2019/10/25/chelsea-stewart-letter-to-dad-payne-stewart.html Warning: You will need lots of tissues!

Letters create a connection, inspire our growth, and move us. I remember attending our Texas SHRM State Council meeting when our guest speaker and board member, Jimmy Taylor, talked about the importance of employee engagement. Toward the end of the meeting, Jimmy challenged all of the attendees to take out our phones, send a personal note to someone who is making an impact in our lives, and say, "Thank you." He stressed to not just say thank you, but to be specific and sincere. Many times, we take it for granted that someone knows what they mean to us and how they are positively impacting our journey. We also take it for granted that we will always have the time to let them know. But we never really know how much time we will have to share our gratitude. We are often so busy in the workplace and with our personal lives that we miss the opportunity to share with others what they have meant to us in our lives.

So today, I want to continue Jimmy's challenge, and challenge you to invest 10-15 minutes to write a letter to someone who inspires you, or someone you appreciate. Be intentional. It can be done on paper or through text, email, or social media. There is power in a letter.

Recently I made a donation to a young boy named Luke, who was selling lemonade. A few weeks later, I received a thank you note from him in the mail. It read, *"Thank you so much for the donation. It means a lot to me. Luke"* That's it! It was specific, sincere, inspiring, and powerful, and most importantly - it made me smile. Don't you think our world needs more smiles? So stop now, and make the investment to put a smile on someone's face. There is power in a personal letter. It will absolutely make someone's day, and it will make your day too! So, who is it going to be? A friend, a family member, a colleague, a supervisor, a volunteer, or possibly someone you don't know personally, who writes and creates content for growth and inspiration for you?

70/30 CHALLENGE

As you read, Frank Blake sent 100 personal notes per week for 7 years, which resulted in over 25,000 personal notes to employees, family, and friends. Why not us? Why not put some good into the world with the "power of the pen?"

> It's time for the "70/30" personal note challenge.
>
> Write 70 notes in 30 days.
>
> Week 1 – Write one note per day.
>
> Week 2 – Write two notes per day.
>
> Week 3 – Write three notes per day.
>
> Week 4 – Write four notes per day.

That's 70 notes in 30 days for a 100 percent investment in people. The notes can be mailed or it can be completed electronically through a LinkedIn recommendation, a book review, an encouraging note for a team member, or a thank you note to your boss, client, family member or friend.

If you choose this challenge, be sure to hold yourself accountable for making sure it is completed each day for the next 30 days.

"I figured the advantage of this is that it created an atmosphere of people being on the lookout for recognizing great behavior." -Frank Blake

SHARE THE GLORY CHALLENGE

In his book, *The Score Takes Care of Itself,* Coach Bill Walsh shares a story about "sharing the glory." He shares his experience from when he was an assistant coach for the Cleveland Browns. During the games, the offensive coordinator (Coach Walsh) would call the plays down to the head coach (Coach Brown) in the headset, then coach Brown would tell the quarterback the offensive play. In interviews after the games, Coach Brown would say that he "chose" or "decided" the play that ended up winning the game. He never gave credit to or mentioned the guy who was actually calling the plays that helped the team win.

After experiencing this type of leadership, Coach Walsh decided that he would never make his assistants feel this way. He would make sure people knew the value they were bringing to the organization. Coach Walsh later became the head coach of the San Francisco 49ers, winner of five Superbowl championships.

When we share the glory, we elevate our leadership. When we receive the credit, we feel more valued and strive to keep getting better. When asked about advice, I always talk about the importance of surrounding yourself with the right people. The right people will share the glory, and make you feel like a valued member of the team. Many times, we might wonder why we are in difficult situations in the workplace, and it is often challenging if we don't feel valued. However, like Coach Walsh's experience, this may be an opportunity to learn how to deal with adversity and the important lesson of "how NOT to lead."

Since writing my book, *Find Your Lane*, people often ask me how we know when we have found our lane, or when we need to make a lane change. I always start with the people. When we are surrounded by people who include us, encourage us, and share the glory, the opportunities are endless. Look around…who is leading you? And more importantly, who are you leading?

How can you share the glory? Here are 10 ideas to get you started:

1. Walk up to someone on your team and let them know something they are doing that is adding value.
2. Send a note to your service partner(s) and let them know how much you appreciate their partnership and the value they bring each day. (This has made my day on more than one occasion.)
3. Post a note on LinkedIn or Twitter and tag your network.
4. If you know someone who has written a book, post a review on Amazon. Once I published my book, *Find Your Lane*, and later *Milemarkers*, I got to experience how it feels. It is very encouraging. Reading those reviews created special moments for me…truly milemarkers!
5. Write a personal note to someone on your team. My boss has been doing this since I joined the Armstrong team in 2004. He always shares the glory with his team. This is one of the reasons I have been at Armstrong for 16 years!
6. Share a quote and tag someone. Let them know you are inspired by them.
7. How about writing a LinkedIn recommendation - without someone asking? It's *Powerful!*
8. Share someone's post on social media. People love to know their posts are valued so much that we want to share them with others.
9. Have a "Post It Note" day and ask everyone to post a note in a dedicated area.
10. Write a note and send it to someone's boss, letting them know the person is going above and beyond.

PODCAST CHALLENGE

Listen to a podcast each week for 30 days and share at least one takeaway each week. You see, when we help people up the mountain, we also get closer to the top!

In the spirit of sharing, here is a recent takeaway I noted from the John Maxwell leadership podcast on "Questions I Ask Myself as a Leader."

1. Am I investing in me? (Personal Growth)
2. Am I genuinely interested in others? (Motive Question)
3. Am I doing what I love and loving what I do? (Passion Question)
4. Am I investing time in the right people? (Relationship Question)
5. Am I staying in my strength zone? (Effectiveness Question)
6. Am I taking others to a higher level? (Mission Question)
7. Am I taking care of today? (Success Question)
8. Am I taking time to think? (Leadership Question)
9. Am I developing leaders? (Legacy Question)
10. Am I pleasing God? (Eternity question)

Focused questions stimulate creative thinking. This is why I enjoy connecting with high performers on *Life in the Leadership Lane*. It's inspiring to reflect on what matters most today. Print a copy of these questions and post them so you can review each day. What question would you add to the list?

Consider adding this final challenge: Think of someone who could move to the next level with some encouragement from you, and reach out to encourage them today.

"*When we encourage others, we are encouraged*!" Bruce Waller

There are so many more challenges. It's not about where you are now, but where you are "growing!" What challenges have you experienced that have helped you to grow as a leader? Send me a note to bruceww300@yahoo.com. I would enjoy hearing your story.

"*Love is the force that ignites the spirit and binds teams together.*"
Phil Jackson

What challenge are you going to accept?

Who are you going to reach out to, to invite to join you?

When one chapter ends, a new one begins. Now is the time to begin your new chapter, living life in the leadership lane. I want to challenge you to review the book and find something you can apply in your career. Don't try to do everything, just one thing from the list below.

1. You're on the air – show up ready to go.
2. Select a day each month to focus on growth.
3. Speak your influence by developing relationships.
4. Drive your brand with purpose.
5. Build your network.
6. Find a way to add more value in your role.
7. Lean into gratitude when failing.
8. Find something to automate and build a habit.
9. Find someone to believe in and make sure they know.
10. Share some of the Five Star Advice with others.

Now it's time to pull over, as we have come to the end of the show. You are now driving in the leadership lane and I want to personally thank you for joining me on this journey and being part of this amazing leadership community. I also want to encourage you to keep going. Life in the leadership lane is not an easy drive, but it's the most amazing trip you will take in your career. It will help you to change the workplace and the world! It's your time, I believe in you!

ACKNOWLEDGEMENTS

Special thanks to all of my former and future guests and everyone in the *Life in the Leadership Lane* podcast community. This includes everyone who has watched and/or listened to the show and provided feedback with a review, a social media post, a text, or in conversations with others. I am a better leader because of you, and I look forward to continued growth with purposeful conversations that make a difference in the workplace and in our community. Together, we can all move leaders to inspire and change the workplace - one conversation at a time.

This book would not have been possible without an incredible community of support. Special thanks to Stacy Davis for helping me give this book life with your countless hours of editing, emails, texts, and commitment to drive this book with purpose. Thank you, Deanne Vick, for bringing your expertise once again with a book cover design, layout and formatting that bring simplicity, clarity, and energy for the reader. Thank you, Allison Rezentes – your photo gave it the final touch.

My network is definitely my net worth, and I am thankful for all of the people involved with both the podcast and book. There are so many people to thank, but it all starts with my friend Katlin Stringer. Thank you for your creativity and inspiration to help me start the podcast including the cover art and all things around *Life in the Leadership Lane*. I will always be grateful for your support!

I also know that it takes a championship team of readers to get a book "over the line" and it wouldn't be possible without your commitment and the time you invested in reading and sharing your perspective. You are all lifters in my life, and I am grateful to have each of you on my team: Jill Cole, Toby Rowland, Bronwyn Allen, Diane Sanford, Tonya Carruthers, Lynne Stewart, Elizabeth Jee, Rose Ann Garza, Dr Sandra Reid, Annie Carolla, Ed Curtis, Lynn Shotwell, Halima K. McWilliams, Lauren Truelove, LaToya Whatley, Adrianne Court, Erin McKelvey, Nicole Roberts, Kelvin Goss, Deborah Reynolds and Deanna Huff.
All of you are high performers, lifters, and inspirations in my life, and I will always be grateful to be carpooling in the leadership lane with you.

Mark Waller - Thank you, brother! When I asked you to write the foreword to *Life in the Leadership Lane*, I knew it would be great - I just didn't realize how great it would be. It's perfect! We have enjoyed some special moments in the leadership lane. I will forever be grateful for all of the opportunities and support you have provided, and more importantly for believing in me. I'm a better leader because of you.

And to my family, Dana, Adam, Alexia, Allison, Chase, Logan, Crosby and Sutton --- You all get 5 stars in my book! You are my WHY and my every day, and I love you more than you know.

SOURCES

CHAPTER 1`

1. Maxwell, John. Maximum Impact Club. Retrieved from audio cassette, 1998.
2. SHRM. Society of Human Resources https://shrm.org/
3. Sinek, Simon. Start with Why. Portfolio, 2009.
4. McWilliams, Halima K., Interview *Life in the Leadership Lane* podcast. Episode 40.
5. Richards, Jimmy, Interview *Life in the Leadership Lane* podcast. Episode 68.
6. Nadella, Satya. Hit Refresh. Harper Collins, 2017.
7. Browne, Steve. Interview *Life in the Leadership Lane* podcast. Episode 48.
8. Freeman, Yvonne. Interview *Life in the Leadership Lane* podcast. Episode 15.
9. Kelleher, Herb. Remembering names. Retrieved from https://www.carminegallo.com/the-power-in-remembering-names/
10. Blake, Frank. 25,000 Letters. Retrieved from https://www.inc.com/elisa-boxer/home-depots-ceo-did-this-25000-times-science-says-you-should-do-it-too.html
11. Chapman, Bob. Everybody Matters. Portfolio, 2015.
12. BrainyQuote. George W. Bush. Quote retrieved from https://www.brainyquote.com/quotes/george_w_bush_386156#:~:text=Bush%20Quotes&text=Please%20enable%20Javascript-,I%20have%20a%20different%20vision%20of%20leadership.,someone%20who%20brings%20people%20together
13. Ziglar, Zig. Prime the Pump retrieved from attended motivational conference. Dallas, Texas. 2009.

CHAPTER 2

1. Dawson, Kevin. Interview *Life in the Leadership Lane* podcast. Episode 1.
2. Hawks, Greg. Interview *Life in the Leadership Lane* podcast. Episode 2.
3. Kallas, Ray. Interview *Life in the Leadership Lane* podcast. Episode 21.
4. Kenny Chesney and Mindy Smith. "*Better Boat*" from *Songs for the Saints*. Blue Chair Warner Brothers Nashville, 2018. Lyrics retrieved from https://www.google.com/search?q=better+boat+lyrics&rlz=1C1GCEV_enUS945US945&oq=better+boat+lyrics&aqs=chrome..69i57.7310j0j9&sourceid=chrome&ie=UTF-8
5. Beckman, Mitch. Interview *Life in the Leadership Lane* podcast. Episode 22.
6. C25K app https://www.c25kfree.com/

7. Sinek, Simon. *The Lifestyle of an Infinite Mindset*. Retrieved from https://www.youtube.com/watch?v=UY-1-9ObaLE

8. Gitomer, Jeffrey. The New Normal Course. Retrieved at https://jeffreygitomer.mykajabi.com/offers/3GP5z2Mf/checkout

9. Burchard, Brendon. *Growth Day* course. Retrieved at https://www.growthday.com/courses-trial

10. Myers, Suzanne. Interview *Life in the Leadership Lane* podcast. Episode 41.

11. Armstrong Relocation www.armstrongrelocation.com

12. Toastmasters International. https://www.toastmasters.org/

13. Wikipedia. Tom Brady. Retrieved from https://en.wikipedia.org/wiki/Tom_Brady

14. Waller, Bruce. Speaker, Lake Dallas High School football team breakfast 2019.

15. *How Lincoln Riley became football's unlikeliest QB guru.* Retrieved from https://www.espn.com/college-football/story/_/id/27356228/how-lincoln-riley-became-football-unlikeliest-qb-guru

16. Gonzalez, Gian Paul. *All In* concept retrieved from North Texas Relocation Professionals Meeting. Frisco, Texas 2019.

17. Rooney, Erica. Interview *Life in the Leadership Lane* podcast. Episode 54.

18. Whatley, LaToya. Interview *Life in the Leadership Lane* podcast. Episode 35.

19. Maxwell, John. *The 21 Irrefutable Laws of Leadership*. Thomas Nelson, 1998.

20. Maxwell, John. Leadership podcast. *Minute with Maxwell* online videos.

21. Itzler, Jesse. *Living with A Seal,* Center Street, 2016.

22. Goals vs. Growth Focus retrieved from listening to *John Maxwell leadership podcast.*

CHAPTER 3

1. Tate, Camille. Interview *Life in the Leadership Lane* podcast. Episode 13.

2. Toastmasters International Club. Dallas, Texas.

3. Find Your Lane, Bruce Waller, 2017.

4. McClure, Jennifer. Interview with Bruce Waller. *Impact Makers* podcast, Episode 31.

5. Sanford, Diane. Interview *Life in the Leadership Lane* podcast. Episode 20.

6. 2020 The HRSouthwest Conference, www.hrsouthwest.com.

7. Cole, Jill. Interview *Life in the Leadership Lane* podcast. Episode 45.

8. Hotlz, Lou. 3 Rules of Life. Retrieved from https://harveymackay.com/lou-holtzs-3-rules-of-life/

9. Myers, Suzanne. Interview *Life in the Leadership Lane* podcast. Episode 41.

10. *Jerry McGuire* Cameron Crowe. TriStar Pictures, 1996.

11. Windley, David. Interview *Life in the Leadership Lane* podcast. Episode 7.

12. *WIIFM.* Dale Carnegie training class. Retrieved from attending in Dallas, Texas, 2002.
13. McColley, Seth. Interview *Life in the Leadership Lane* podcast. Episode 5.
14. *25 words to avoid in sales* https://www.newbreedrevenue.com/blog/words-to-avoid-in-your-sales-pitch
15. Hanks, Tom. American actor and filmmaker. Retrieve from watching Academy Awards speech.
16. Goss, Kelvin. Interview *Life in the Leadership Lane* podcast. Episode 14.
17. McKeown, Greg. *Essentialism.* Crown Publishing Group, 2020.
18. Crews, Dr. Derek. Interview *Life in the Leadership Lane* podcast. Episode 61.

CHAPTER 4

1. Son, Jamie. Interview *Life in the Leadership Lane* podcast. Episode 28.
2. Daues, Lianne. Interview *Life in the Leadership Lane* podcast. Episode 47.
3. Zoller, Kim. Interview *Life in the Leadership Lane* podcast. Episode 39.
4. McClure, Jennifer. Personal Brand Workbook, https://jennifermcclure.net/2018/08/16/taking-your-personal-brand-to-the-next-level-with-jennifer-mcclure/
5. Dorsey, Justin. Interview *Life in the Leadership Lane* podcast. Episode 64.
6. Hsieh, Tony. *Delivering Happiness.* Grand Central Publishing, 2010.
7. Wikipedia. *Drive To Survive* https://en.wikipedia.org/wiki/Formula_1:_Drive_to_Survive
8. Domino's pizza "brand promotion" retrieved from https://www.businessinsider.com/dominos-free-pizza-russia-tattoos-promo-ends-early-2018-9.
9. Ohio-based restaurant MELT "brand promotion" retrieved from https://meltbarandgrilled.com/the-melt-experience/the-tattoo-family/
10. Texas Relocation Conference. Carrollton, Texas, 2020.
11. Gladwell, Malcolm. *Outliers,* Little Brown and Company, 2008.
12. Heath, Chip and Dan. *The Power of Moments.* Simon and Schuster, 2017.
13. Goebel, Melissa. Interview *Life in the Leadership Lane* podcast. Episode 43.
14. Singletary, Mike. BrainyQuote. Retrieved from https://www.brainyquote.com/quotes/mike_singletary_127505
15. TalentNet Live Conference. Dallas, Texas 2018. https://talentnetlive.com/
16. Goodreads. Rohn, Jim. Retrieved from https://www.goodreads.com/quotes/855377-the-bigger-the-why-the-easier-the-how#:~:text=Quote%20by%20Jim%20Rohn%3A%20%E2%80%9CThe,easier%20the%20'how'.%E2%80%9D

CHAPTER 5

1. Shaw, Angela. Interview *Life in the Leadership Lane* podcast. Episode 8.
2. Allen, Bronwyn. Interview *Life in the Leadership Lane* podcast. Episode 71.
3. Blakely, Sarah. Quote retrieved listening to Darren Hardy *Success* CD.
4. Collins, Lisa. Interview *Life in the Leadership Lane* podcast. Episode 53.
5. Leadership LINKS, DallasHR Leadership Development Program 2015. www.DallasHR.org
6. Maxwell, John. Retrieved interview with John Wooden https://youtu.be/eKMNjN3n_sc
7. Stoops, Bob. Interview *Life in the Leadership Lane* podcast. Episode 72.
8. Stoops, Bob / Wojciechowski, Gene. *No Excuses: The Making of a Head Coach*. Little Brown and Company, 2019.
9. HBC Champions Foundation https://hbcchampionsfoundation.com/
10. The HRSouthwest Conference. www.hrsouthwest.com
11. Brown, Brene. Dare to Lead. Random House Publishing, 2018.
12. CLIMB book club. Online Facebook Group.
13. Carolla, Annie. Interview *Life in the Leadership Lane* podcast. Episode 23.
14. Miller, Mark. The Heart of Leadership. Read How You Want, 2013.
15. Sinek, Simon. Start with Why. Portfolio, 2009.
16. TED. Simon Sinek: The Golden Circle. Retrieved from https://www.ted.com/talks/simon_sinek_how_great_leaders_inspire_action?language=en
17. Texas SHRM, www.texasshrm.org
18. Windley, David. Interview *Life in the Leadership Lane* podcast. Episode 6.
19. Pisciotta, Kim. Interview *Life in the Leadership Lane* podcast. Episode 54.
20. Mobility" magazine, WorldwideERC. https://www.worldwideerc.org/mobility-magazine
21. Find Your Lane, Bruce Waller, 2017.
22. Mosley, Shannon. Interview *Life in the Leadership Lane* podcast. Episode 42.
23. Rooney, Erica. Interview *Life in the Leadership Lane* podcast. Episode 57.

CHAPTER 6

1. Atkinson, Jane, The Wealthy Speaker 2.0, The Proven Formula for building your successful speaking business, 2012, Jane Atkinson 2nd ed.
2. Carruthers, Tonya. Interview *Life in the Leadership Lane* podcast. Episode *55.*
3. Clark, Clark. Interview *Life in the Leadership Lane* podcast. Episode 56.
4. Browne, Steve. *HR On Purpose*, Society for Human Resource Management, 2017.
5. Crews, Dr. Derek. *Mastering Human Resource Management*. FlatWorld, 2021.

6. Sarraille, Mike and Randle, George. *The Talent War*. Lioncrest Publishing, 2020.

7. Bridwell, Tony. *Saturday Morning Tea*. B2B Books, 2020.

8. Rowland, Toby. *Unhitch the Wagon: The Story of Boomer and Sooner*. Ascend Books, 2020.

9. Stoops, Bob / Wojciechowski, Gene. *No Excuses: The Making of a Head Coach*. Little Brown and Company, 2019.

10. Maxwell, John. *21 Irrefutable Laws of Leadership*. Thomas Nelson, 1998.

11. BrainyQuote, Jim Rohn. Retrieved from https://www.brainyquote.com/quotes/jim_rohn_147512#:~:text=Please%20enable%20Javascript,Success%20is%20not%20to%20be%20pursued%3B%20it%20is%20to%20be,by%20the%20person%20you%20become

12. Grant, Adam. *Work Life Podcast*. Retrieved story about Shane Battier on podcast.

13. Hardy, Darren. *Compound Effect*. Vanguard Press, 2012. *"100/0 rule."*

14. BrainyQuote. George Hallas. Retrieved from https://www.brainyquote.com/quotes/george_halas_160094

15. *When The Game Stands Tall*. Thomas Carter. David Zelon. 2014.

16. Lueckemeyer, Paige. Interview *Life in the Leadership Lane* podcast. Episode *25*.

17. Armstrong Relocation Virtual Surveys. www.armstrongrelocation.com

18. Bush, George W. "I Can Hear You" Retrieved from YouTube https://www.youtube.com/watch?v=zi2SNFnfMjk

19. Cunningham, Robert. *A very heroic moment in baseball history, Jim Rice a real hero and baseball story*. Retrieved from https://artstribune.com/2021/03/27/a-very-heroic-moment-in-baseball-history-jim-rice-a-real-hero-and-baseball-story/

CHAPTER 7

1. Stewart, Lynne. Interview *Life in the Leadership Lane* podcast. Episode *9*.

2. McKelvey, Erin. Interview *Life in the Leadership Lane* podcast. Episode 65.

3. Carter, Chris. *A Football Life*. NFL Network, 2011.

4. Carnegie, Dale. Retrieved from sales training program in Dallas, Texas.

5. Maxwell, John. 21 *Irrefutable Laws of Leadership*. Thomas Nelson, 1998.

6. Browne, Steve. Retrieved quote from SHRM National Conference 2019, Las Vegas, Nevada.

7. Johnson M.D., Spencer, *Who Moved My Cheese*. Simon and Schuster, 2009.

8. Hardy, Darren. *The Compound Effect*. Vanguard Press, 2012.

9. Albom, Mitch. *Tuesdays with Morrie*. Doubleday, 2007.

10. Gitomer, Jeffrey. *Little Red Book of Selling*. Bard Press, 2004.

11. Wooden, John. *Game Plan for Success*. McGraw Hill Education, 2009.

12. Waller, Bruce. *Find Your Lane,* Bruce Waller, 2017.

13. Maxwell, John. *The Maxwell Daily Reader*. Thomas Nelson, 2007. "I am."

14. Reid, Dr. Sandra. Quote retrieved by Bruce Waller.

15. Blakely, Sarah. Retrieved interview with Darren hardy on *Success Magazine* CD.

16. Heath, Chip and Dan. *The Power of Moments*. Simon and Schuster, 2017.

17. Wikipedia. *Frequency Illusion, the Baader–Meinhof Phenomenon* Retrieved at https://en.wikipedia.org/wiki/Frequency_illusion#:~:text=Frequency%20ill usion%2C%20also%20known%20as,a%20form%20of%20selection%20bia s).

18. Shaffer, Melanie. Interview *Life in the Leadership Lane* podcast. Episode 30.

19. Brown, Brene. *Dare to Lead.* Random House Publishing, 2018.

20. Armstrong Relocation and Companies www.armstrongrelocation.com

21. Tri City Lanes Story by Bruce Waller.

22. Rezentes, Crosby. *What's in your Blank* retrieved by Bruce Waller.

23. Linebarger, Christie. Interview *Life in the Leadership Lane* podcast. Episode 32.

CHAPTER 8

1. Garza, Rose Ann. Interview *Life in the Leadership Lane* podcast. Episode 17.

2. Ziglar, Zig. Brainy Quote Retrieved from https://www.brainyquote.com/quotes/zig_ziglar_381984

3. Waller, Bruce. *Find Your Lane*, Bruce Waller, 2017.

4. Windley, David. Interview *Life in the Leadership Lane* podcast. Episode 7.

5. Shaffer, Melanie. Interview *Life in the Leadership Lane* podcast. Episode 30.

6. McColley, Seth. Interview *Life in the Leadership Lane* podcast. Episode 5.

7. Stanier, Michael Bungay. *The Coaching Habit.* Page Two, 2016.

8. Zoller, Kim. Interview *Life in the Leadership Lane* podcast. Episode 39.

9. Bogard, Danny. Interview *Life in the Leadership Lane* podcast. Episode 44.

10. Rezentes, Allison. Interview *Life in the Leadership Lane* podcast. Episode 50.

11. Stoops, Bob. Interview *Life in the Leadership Lane* podcast. Episode 72.

12. Tate, Camille. Interview *Life in the Leadership Lane* podcast. Episode 13.

13. Monk, Mandy. Interview *Life in the Leadership Lane* podcast. Episode 37.

14. Myers, Suzanne. Interview *Life in the Leadership Lane* podcast. Episode 41.

15. Mensching, Leslie. Interview *Life in the Leadership Lane* podcast. Episode 34.

16. Melissa Carrillo Interview *Life in the Leadership Lane* podcast. Episode 33.

17. Whatley, LaToya. Interview *Life in the Leadership Lane* podcast. Episode 35.

18. Truelove, Lauren. Interview *Life in the Leadership Lane* podcast. Episode 52.
19. Rooney, Erica. Interview *Life in the Leadership Lane* podcast. Episode 57.
20. Court, Adrianne. Interview *Life in the Leadership Lane* podcast. Episode 27.

CHAPTER 9

1. Sanford, Diane. Interview *Life in the Leadership Lane* podcast. Episode 20.
2. Maxwell, John. Baseball pitcher story retrieved from https://www.johnmaxwell.com/blog/developing-a-powerful-positive-perspective/
3. Cole, Jill. Interview *Life in the Leadership Lane* podcast. Episode 45.
4. Ziglar, Zig. *See You At The Top*. CD. Simon and Schuster, 1974.
5. Gaines, Chip. *No Pain No Gains*. Thomas Nelson, 2021.
6. Holtz, Lou. Audio Book *Wins Losses and Lessons*. HarperAudio, 2006.
7. Goodreads. Rohn, Jim. Quote retrieved from https://www.goodreads.com/quotes/2965423-if-you-want-to-get-more-you-have-to-become
8. Burns, Ken. *Country music: A Film by Ken Burns*. PBS TV, 2019.
9. Song *"Why Not Me"* Wynona and Naomi Judd. Songwriters: Sonny Throckmorton / Harlan Howard / Brent Maher. Why Not Me Album, 1984.
10. Williams, Hank. *I'm So Lonely I Could Cry*. Written by Hank Williams, 1949.
11. Smith, Jessica. *Why We Should All Strive to Be More Like Albert Einstein's Mother*. Retrieved from Odyssey: https://www.theodysseyonline.com/strive-albert-einsteins-mother
12. Bruce Waller. Poem "Find Your Lane.." www.brucewaller.com, 2020.

CHAPTER 10

1. Rezentes, Allison. Interview *Life in the Leadership Lane* podcast. Episode 50.
2. Deputy, Angela. Interview *Life in the Leadership Lane* podcast. Episode 63.
3. Paschal, Dustin. Interview *Life in the Leadership Lane* podcast. Episode 11.
4. Valvano, Jim. *ESPYS* Speech Retrieved from https://youtu.be/HuoVM9nm42E
5. Kechely, Kragen. Retrieved quote from Dallas Baptist University Business Webinar, March 2021.
6. *Saul Gresky*, North Texas Relocation Professionals. www.northtexasrelocationprofessionals.org
7. *The View from the Top*. "The Global Mobility Top 100 Most Admired Service Providers of 2021" at Benivo: https://top100.benivo.com/service-providers-2021

8. Amazon review https://www.amazon.com/Find-Your-Lane-Change-Career/dp/0692865632#:~:text=January%208%2C%202021-,Find%20Your%20Lane%3A%20Change%20your%20GPS%2C%20Change%20your%20Career%20by,uncertainty%20that%20comes%20with%20it.

9. "Brick Wall of Leadership Advice" shared on *Life in the Leadership Lane Interview* Podcasts 1-75. Chrissie Rogers, LaTonya McElroy, Jimmy Taylor, Angela Shaw, Steve Browne, Annie Carolla, Lianne Daues, Jill Cole, Danny Bogard, Mary Leone, Melissa Goebel, Shannon Mosley, Suzanne Myers, Halima K. McWilliams, Kim Zoller, Mandy Monk, Martha E. Thornton, Seth McColley, LaToya Whatley, Tyra Bremer, Dustin Paschal, Greg Hawks, Paige Lueckemeyer, Melissa Carrillo, Kathy Hardcastle, Lynne Stewart, Christie Linebarger, Janet Hanofee, Mitch Beckman, Jamie Son, Rose Ann Garza, Camille Tate, Melanie Shaffer, Yvonne K. Freeman, Diane Sanford, Lynn Shotwell, David Windley, Toby Rowland, Kevin Dawson, Jessica Heer, Ed Curtis, Ray Kallas, Mike Sarraille, George Randle, Denise Snow, Kelvin Goss, Tony Bridwell, Allison Rezentes, Adrianne Court, Erica Rooney, Connie Clark, Tonya Carruthers, Kim Pisciotta, Lisa Collins, Lauren Truelove, Leann Day, Leslie Mensching, Nicole Roberts, Shawn Storer, Bruce Waller, Jennifer Swisher, Dr. Derek Crews, Kim Kneidel, Angela Deputy, Justin Dorsey, Erin McKelvey, Dustin Jones, Nicole DiRocco, Jimmy Richards, Holly Novak, Brian Yanus, Bronwyn Allen, Bob Stoops, Jed Gifford, Adam Waller, Carol Kiburz, Jane Atkinson, Rachel Kennedy.

TAKE THE CHALLENGE

1. Deputy, Angela. Interview *Life in the Leadership Lane* podcast. Episode 63.
2. *Murph Challenge* Retrieved from https://themurphchallenge.com/pages/the-workout
3. *MAUPIN workout*. Retrieved from https://wodwell.com/wod/maupin/
4. "Create Your Name Challenge." Dr. Sandra Reid, Chair of Graduate School of Business at Dallas Baptist University.
5. *Find Your Brand Challenge* Retrieved from jennifermcclure.net
6. Waller, Bruce. *Find Your Lane*. Amazon, 2017.
7. Wikipedia Payne Stewart Plane Crash https://en.wikipedia.org/wiki/Payne_Stewart
8. Stewart, Chelsea. *Miss you every day*. Retrieved from https://www.pgatour.com/long-form/2019/10/25/chelsea-stewart-letter-to-dad-payne-stewart.html
9. Blake, Frank. *Home Depot's CEO did this 25000 times*. Retrieved from https://www.inc.com/elisa-boxer/home-depots-ceo-did-this-25000-times-science-says-you-should-do-it-too.html
10. Walsh, Bill. *The Score Takes Care of Itself*. Portfolio, 2010.

11. John Maxwell *Leadership* Podcast. "Questions I ask myself as a leader." *Retrieve from https://podcasts.apple.com/us/podcast/the-john-maxwell-leadership-podcast/id1416206538*

12. Waller, Bruce. Original Quote.

13. Jackson, Phil. *BrainyQuote.* Retrieved at *https://www.brainyquote.com/quotes/phil_jackson_381751#:~:text=Phil%2 0Jackson%20Quotes&text=Love%20is%20the%20force%20that%20ignites %20the%20spirit%20and%20binds%20teams%20together*

ABOUT THE AUTHOR

Bruce Waller is the Vice President of Corporate Relocation for Armstrong Relocation and Companies in Dallas, Texas. Bruce has enjoyed many roles in relocation from operations to general management for over 25 years, and currently arranges services for organizations that need to relocate talent across the US and abroad. Bruce is a former President and Chairman of the Board for DallasHR, the third largest SHRM chapter in the US, and he currently serves as a Director of Leadership Development for Texas SHRM State Council. Bruce is certified by both HRCI (Human Resources Certification Institute) with a PHR, and SHRM (Society of Human Resource Management) with a SHRM-CP.

Bruce also serves on the North Texas Relocation Professionals Board of Directors and is certified by WorldwideERC as a Certified Relocation Professional (CRP). Bruce is a former recipient of the 2014 Saul Gresky Award presented to NTRP's Relocation Professional of the Year, and has received many awards including UniGroup Masters Club and Armstrong Relocation Presidents Club.

Bruce graduated from the University of Central Oklahoma with a degree in Business Administration.

Bruce writes a weekly blog on Leadership, HR, and Mobility called "Move to Inspire" that you can subscribe to at brucewaller.com. It's a quick, inspirational read to jumpstart your week! He also published two other books - one leadership book called *Find Your Lane* where he uses a "Career GPS" approach to inspire people and help people navigate a career with purpose, and *Milemarkers: A Five Year Journal* where he provides a tool to record your daily highlights and live with more purpose each day.

Bruce is the host of *Life in the Leadership Lane*, a weekly podcast where he interviews leaders making a difference in the workplace. You can find his show on your favorite podcast platform. Be sure and subscribe, post a review, and share with others.

Some fun facts about Bruce... He has bowled 10 perfect 300 games and loves diet coke, peanut butter, and spending time with grandkids Crosby and Sutton!

In 2021, Bruce was selected *Global Mobility Top 100 - The Most Admired Service Providers in 2021* by Benivo, and he received the award for Texas SHRM Volunteer Leader of the Year.

For more information about Bruce Waller, his books and podcast:

- About Bruce https://brucewaller.com/about-bruce/
- LinkedIn https://www.linkedin.com/in/brucewaller/
- Twitter https://twitter.com/BruceWaller
- Facebook https://www.facebook.com/brucewwaller
- Instagram https://www.instagram.com/bruceww300/
- YouTube https://www.youtube.com/channel/UC5P-sgiIWmNp3IDlVzSj0AQ
- Publications:

Find Your Lane and *Milemarkers: A Five-Year Journey*
Available on Amazon and your favorite online bookstore:

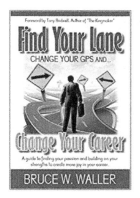 

Life in the Leadership Lane podcast
Available on your favorite podcast platform.